William Shakespeare

THE TRAGEDY OF
KING RICHARD
THE SECOND

New Kittredge Shakespeare

William Shakespeare

THE TRAGEDY OF
KING RICHARD
THE SECOND

Editor
Thomas A. Pendleton
Iona College

Series Editor
James H. Lake
Louisiana State University,
Shreveport

The Tragedy of King Richard the Second
Copyright © 2012 Focus Publishing
Edited by George Lyman Kittredge.
Used with permission from the heirs to the Kittredge estate.
New material by Thomas A. Pendleton used with permission.

Focus Publishing/R. Pullins Company
PO Box 369
Newburyport MA 01950
www.pullins.com

Cover Design by Guy Wetherbee | Elk Amino Design, New England | elkaminodesign@yahoo.com

Cover: King Richard stops the duel between the dukes of Hereford and Norfolk. Color lithograph, 1864 © Duncan Walker / iStock Photo.

ISBN: 978-1-58510-179-5

To see available eBook versions, visit www.pullins.com

Library of Congress Cataloging-in-Publication Data

Shakespeare, William, 1564-1616.
  [King Richard II]
  The tragedy of King Richard the second / William Shakespeare ; editor,
Thomas A. Pendleton.
    p. cm. -- (New Kittredge Shakespeare)
  Includes bibliographical references.
  ISBN 978-1-58510-179-5
  1. Richard II, King of England, 1367-1400--Drama. 2. Great
Britain--History--Richard II, 1377-1399--Drama. I. Pendleton, Thomas A. II.
Kittredge, George Lyman, 1960-1941. III. Title.
  PR2820.A2P36 2012
  822.3'3--dc23
                          2012010862

Printed in the United States of America

10 9 8 7 6 5 4 3 2 1

0312V

TABLE OF CONTENTS

Publisher's Note

George Lyman Kittredge was one of the foremost American Shakespeare scholars of the 20th century. The New Kittredge Shakespeare builds on his celebrated scholarship and extensive notes. Each edition contains a new, updated introduction, with comments on contemporary film versions of the play, an essay on reading the play as performance, and topics for discussion, with an annotated bibliography and filmography. For this an accomplished Shakespeare and film scholar has been commissioned to modernize each volume.

The series focuses on understanding the language and allusions in the play, as well as encountering Shakespeare as performance. The audience ranges from students at all levels to readers interested in encountering the text in the context of its performance on stage or on film.

Ron Pullins, Publisher
Newburyport, 2009

INTRODUCTION TO THE KITTREDGE EDITION[1]

The Tragedy of King Richard the Second

For *Richard the Second* the First Quarto (1597) furnishes a good text, which, except for the abdication scene (4.1.154–318), is the basis of the present edition. Later Quartos date from 1598 (two), 1608, and 1615, each being set up from its immediate predecessor. For the First Folio a copy of the Fifth Quarto (1615) seems to have been used. The abdication scene was published for the first time in the Fourth Quarto (1608). Its omission from the earlier Quartos was probably due to official censorship or to the publishers' fear of prosecution. At all events, it was manifestly present in the drama as originally written. The Quarto text is defective and corrupt in the abdication scene, but the Folio affords most of the necessary corrections.

Style and blank verse put *Richard the Second* close to the time of *King John*. Which came first is doubtful, but *King John* is probably the older; for it would have been more natural for Shakespeare to pass on to *Henry IV* after writing *Richard the Second* than to turn back two hundred years for his next historical subject. This consideration outweighs the argument that, since *Richard the Second* belongs to the so-called 'lyrical group' and *King John* does not, *Richard the Second* must be the earlier, inasmuch as Shakespeare would never have returned to his lyrical manner after he had once abandoned it. But Shakespeare was surely capable of lyricism at any period, and, though he dropped this manner in *King John*, there is no reason why he should not have resumed it under the compulsion of a theme so essentially lyrical as the character and misfortunes of King Richard. If, as is possible, he had written *A Midsummer Night's Dream* in the interval, the lyric manner of *Richard the Second* may well have been influenced thereby. Reasonable dates, then, are 1594 for *King John*, early in 1595 for *A Midsummer Night's Dream*, and late in 1595 or early in 1596 for *Richard the Second*.

Parallels between *Richard the Second* and Samuel Daniel's poem on *The Civil Wars* have been cited as evidence for 1595 as a date for the play, but these prove nothing. Quite as elusive is the testimony of a letter written by Sir Edward Hoby on December 7, 1595, to invite Sir Robert Cecil to his house in Canon Row, Westminster, on the

---

1   EDITORS' NOTE: Kittredge's Introduction, with its discussion of Shakespeare's complex adaptation of sources, is largely unchanged. I have added explanatory footnotes and some clarifications.

9th, "where as late as it shal please you a gate for your supper shal be open: & K. Richard present him selfe to your vewe." If Hoby was referring to a dramatic entertainment (as may or may not be the case), nothing proves that he had Shakespeare's play in mind, for there were other dramas in existence dealing with the same reign; nor is it certain that some *Richard the Third* was not the piece in question.

For his historical materials Shakespeare used the second edition of Holinshed's *Chronicle* (1587). Perhaps he took a hint now and then from other easily accessible books. The pretty story about "roan Barbary," for instance (5.5.78 ff.), may have been suggested by what is told about the king's grey-hound by Froissart, whom Shakespeare doubtless knew in Berners's translation. Froissart is mentioned in *1 Henry VI*. The garden scene (3.4) and the parting of Richard and his queen (5.1) are Shakespeare's own. The time covered by the action is so short that no such chronological vagaries are to be expected. The play opens on April 29, 1398; on September 16, Bolingbroke and Mowbray met in the lists at Coventry and were banished; Bolingbroke landed at Ravenspurgh in June or July, 1399; King Richard was deposed on September 30 in the same year and was murdered at Pomfret Castle in January, 1400.

The connection of *Richard the Second* with Essex's rebellion in 1601 is a matter of curious interest but has no literary significance, except as showing the popularity of the play. When Essex was tried in 1600 for his acts in Ireland, his fondness for this play was part of the evidence against him; and *Richard the Second* was played at the Globe, at the instance of his partisans, on the day before the outbreak.

Because *Richard the Second* does not maintain an absolutely uniform standard of excellence in style and metre, critics have suspected that Shakespeare utilized some lost play on the subject and kept fragments of the old text without change. There is not much to be said in favor of any such theory.

Though *Richard the Second* is not Marlowesque in style, Shakespeare was undoubtedly influenced by Marlowe's *Edward II* in his choice of a subject; and there is more or less resemblance between his Richard and Marlowe's Edward. Both are weak, impulsive, and self-willed, and both are governed by unworthy favorites. But Marlowe's king is worse than frivolous; he is frankly despicable. He has neither the poetic nature nor the imaginative intensity of Shakespeare's Richard. There is no comparison between the plays in the matter of pathos and emotional sway.

George Lyman Kittredge

INTRODUCTION TO THE FOCUS EDITION

Richard II ruled England for almost twenty-two years, but Shakespeare's play deals with only the last two of his reign and his life. In this, Shakespeare follows Edward Hall's chronicle history of 1548: like Hall, he begins with the quarrel between Bolingbroke and Mowbray, and like Hall, he sees the quarrel as the critical first step leading to Richard's deposition and death, which itself led to almost 100 years of disastrous history for England.

Shakespeare's play hints frequently at his intention to continue the story beyond Richard. Perhaps most clearly, Richard's prediction of conflict between Bolingbroke and his supporter Northumberland (5.1.55-68) will be borne out in the action of the next play in the sequence, *Henry IV, Part One*, and Bolingbroke's worries about his "unthrifty son" (5.3.1-22) will foretell Prince Hal's dalliance in the tavern world in both *Henry IV* plays. But in a curious way, *Richard II* looks both back and forward at the same time; the disasters the Bishop of Carlisle eloquently predicts (4.1.114-49) would, of course, occur in future historical time, but they had also already occurred in past theatrical time, since Shakespeare had already dramatized them in the *Henry VI* plays and *Richard III*. In fact, without these plays of the First Tetralogy, it is difficult to imagine that Shakespeare would have gone back to dramatize the earlier history that preceded them, starting with *Richard II*.

This play is structured on the fall of Richard and the complementary rise of his cousin and successor, Henry Bolingbroke, who becomes King Henry IV. Between Richard, king as the play begins, and Bolingbroke, king as it ends, Shakespeare arranges a considerable number of parallels and oppositions. Bolingbroke in Act 4, scene 1 presides over challenges among his nobles, as Richard had in the first act. Richard's appropriation of Bolingbroke's inheritance in Act 2, scene 1 is followed by three malcontents plotting against him; Bolingbroke's deposition of Richard in Act 4, scene 1 is followed by three malcontents plotting to overthrow him. Bolingbroke's return from exile in Act 2, scene 3, after almost 500 lines of absence from the play, is greeted by a succession of arrivals, all of whom bring support and good news. Richard's return from Ireland in Act 3, scene 2, after somewhat more than 500 lines of absence, is met by a comparable series of messages, now all extremely bad news.

With these returns, the characters of the two antagonists change significantly. The Richard of the opening scenes is increasingly unsympathetic. He is frivolous, arbitrary, amazingly callous on hearing of Gaunt's impending death; and his appropriating Bolingbroke's inheritance is classically the deed of a tyrant who sets aside all considerations of law, custom, and equity in favor of his own will. On the other hand, Bolingbroke seems brave and patriotic; he is a loving son; and his grievance against Mowbray appears justifiable.

The Bolingbroke who returns, however, is largely an enigma. Apart from a couple of apparently sincere outbursts of indignation at his mistreatment, his motives are continually ambiguous. He and his supporters regularly claim that he has returned from exile only to claim the inheritance that Richard has unjustly denied him, and as late as the Flint Castle scene, he represents himself as ready to resume his loyal obedience to the King. But, since Shakespeare never gives him a soliloquy, we cannot help but question whether his professed purposes are his real purposes. Bolingbroke clearly exceeds his authority in executing Bushy and Green, and he seems never to reflect on the consequences of his imposing his own will on Richard, although Richard himself responds as if his deposition were now a *fait accompli*. As readers or audience, we learn of that deposition very much at second hand, as Richard's Queen does, from the conversation of the gardeners, by which time it is something that "every one doth know." But we never learn how that decision was made and what part Bolingbroke had in it. And even when Exton reports Bolingbroke's wish for Richard's death (Act 5, scene 4), we are given hearsay, not the actual context in which he spoke, so that Bolingbroke's final sorrowful acceptance of responsibility for the murder may be read as either genuine or hypocritical.

Two plays later, in *Henry IV, Part Two*, Bolingbroke, now an old and sickly king, reflects on Richard's deposition and claims "Though then, God knows, I had no such intent,/ But that necessity so bow'd the state/ That I and greatness were compell'd to kiss." This might be the truth of the matter, though even this can be read as self-justification; and, of course, these lines do not occur in *Richard II*. Bolingbroke can be, and often is, read by critics and played by actors both as a thorough Machiavellian, and equally as well as one who has had fortune thrust upon him. Shakespeare never gives us the basis for a definitive answer, and since he easily could have done so, his intention seems to have been to keep Bolingbroke's interiority opaque.

With the Richard who returns from his Irish expedition, however, things could hardly be more different. From this point on, what Richard thinks, feels, hopes, and fears becomes the increasing focus of the play's attention, and of its sympathy. When he returns in Act 3, scene 2, his earlier recklessness now transforms itself into an instability that oscillates repeatedly between announcements of his divinely guaranteed inviolability to assertions of the hopelessness of his situation. He constructs remarkable fantasies of the very land animating itself to repel his enemies and of his mere appearance reducing Bolingbroke to terrified flight. Yet within 20 lines of proclaiming that God will at need lend him legions of angels, he recommends that "All souls that will be safe, fly from my side."(3.2.80). For Richard, both the image of his own transcendent majesty and the role of regal victim are equally, if alternately, attractive. The word *role* suggests a view of Richard often proposed—usually by unsympathetic readers—of

Richard as the player king, heedless of the practical realities of his situation and obsessed with posing, with striking attitudes, with projecting a persona. There is point to this reaction, for Richard, except for his scene in prison, always has an on-stage audience, and on a number of occasions, he explicitly comments on their reactions to him. It is probably accurate to say that he is always at least implicitly concerned with how his projections of himself are received by those present to witness them. Indeed there are moments in the play when Richard himself seems to have withdrawn to become his own observer, even to his fantasizing a future that will memorialize his pathetic end: his queen, for example, will surpass the saddest of all sad stories with "the lamentable tale of me" (5.1.44). But Richard as player king is by no means the totality of the character, for however histrionically and hyperbolically he portrays himself, his experience, which is increasingly the experience of suffering, is real. However self-pitying, narcissistic, even solipsistic Richard may be, the continual exploration of his interiority ultimately demands some element of sympathy for the pain he undergoes.

What comes considerably closer to the truth than Richard as player king is the comparable portrayal—now usually by sympathetic readers—of Richard as poet king. This must be understood as romantic poet some centuries before Wordsworth, because Richard's subject is always himself. What his speeches repeatedly present are his own occasional exultation and his increasingly frequent despair, anger, and outrage, often expressed in notably eloquent and evocative language. Much like the mythic poet of *A Midsummer Night's Dream*, Richard's imagination gives the airy nothings of his shifting feeling-states local habitations and names, often of remarkable poetic quality.

Especially notable in this regard are the images Richard creates so abundantly to particularize moments of these feeling states. During the confrontation at Flint Castle, he casts himself as Phaeton, "wanting the manage of unruly jades" (3.3.179); during the deposition scene, he imagines the crown he surrenders to Bolingbroke as a well with "two buckets, filling one another" (4.1.185); and later in the scene, he longs for annihilation, like "a mockery king of snow" melting under "the sun of Bolingbroke" (4.1.260-61). These are brief, almost momentary images; even more impressive, however, are the extended metaphoric conceits that structure a number of Richard's finest speeches. In his initial exultation, he likens himself on his return from Ireland to the sun, "the searching eye of heaven," rising over "the proud tops of the eastern pines" to scatter the evil things of night, exactly as his own brilliance will confound

> this thief, this traitor, Bolingbroke,
> Who all this while hath reveled in the night
> Whilst we were wand'ring with the Antipodes.   (3.2.47-49)

Even more striking is Richard's imaginative creation of the antic Death, who resides "within the mortal temples of a king," allows him "a little scene,/ To monarchize, be feared and kill with looks," but "Comes at the last and with a little pin/ Bores through the castle wall, and farewell king!" (3.2.165-70).

However useful it is to think of Richard as poet king, he is of course actually a character in a poetic drama, and one in which everyone always speaks in verse and often in rhyme. Still within the play, with Bolingbroke closed off to us, it is only Richard's interiority, his consciousness that is presented to us and gives us access to the human experience of the political reversals. Although Richard's shortcomings as king are not refuted, another claim on our sympathy begins to assert itself. The language in which this claim is presented bespeaks human qualities like sensitivity, intelligence, speed and variety of thought, intensity of feeling, and a deep sense of loss. Our valuing the quality of the language inevitably entails some valuing at least of the implied character from whom it issues. In this, Richard's portrayal of his own experience is at times especially poignant or striking or memorable as the language of an autonomous poem might be. His appeal is perhaps greatest when he asserts the common humanity he shares with the audience: Richard closes the great "of comfort no man speak" with

> I live with bread like you, feel want,
> Taste grief, need friends; subjected thus,
> How can you say to me I am a king?   (3.2.175-77)

The impression of directness and sincerity created by the surrounding monosyllables provides a validating setting for the elegant pun on "subjected." The linguistic detail that achieves the effect is properly Shakespeare's, the author's, but the effect itself comments on who and what Richard is, above and beyond his shortcomings as king.

However powerfully such a moment evokes the common humanity that Richard shares with his audience, it is at least equally important that Richard is different: he is unique because he is the king. However unfamiliar the concept of kingship may appear to us—especially as 21st century Americans—for both Richard's age and Shakespeare's, it was a near universal assumption that monarchy was the natural and appropriate form of government. The king thus symbolized and concretized in his person that which his society valued, even reverenced, most. The king's position as governor, judge, and law giver was at least in theory beyond dispute, and his entitlement to loyalty, obedience, deference, and even love tended to be supported in religious terms. The king was king by God's determination, and thus to oppose him was not merely treason, but sacrilege as well. The extreme of this kind of thinking is found most often in Richard's own speeches, although Carlisle also has an eloquent speech on the divine right of the king during the deposition scene, and as early as the play's second scene, Gaunt announces that, even to avenge his own brother's death, he would not raise "An angry arm" against the King, "God's substitute,/ His deputy anointed in his sight." (1.2.37-38).

What seems most relevant here is Richard's own belief in his kingship, not only that it justifies who he is and what he is owed, but also that without it, Richard feels that he has no identity: "I have no name, no title–/ No, not that name was given me at the font–/But 'tis usurp'd." (4.1.255-57). This is the essentially paradoxical state that the deposition forces upon him: he is renouncing what he holds to be impossible to renounce; he is ex-king, non-king, and yet still king, all at the same time. Under these contradictory pressures, Richard's performance during the deposition scene is remarkable and mercurial, as he moves from ironic poses to bitter and direct condemnations to the virtual creation of a deposition ceremony to self-indulgent lamentation, all as some action or some word calls forth his quick and surprisingly inventive response. His repeated comparisons of his own ordeal with Christ's may strike the hearer as moving or blasphemous, but it seems as if we are intended to accept that Richard finds the analogy valid.

The Richard of the prison soliloquy seems perhaps somewhat wiser and more resigned, but he is by no means totally changed. For once without an audience, he attempts to imaginatively create one to people the world of his mind. He is now sufficiently appreciative to recognize the devotion of the Groom and of whoever it was that arranged for the music he hears, but he remains self-pitying enough to characterize it as "a strange brooch in this all-hating world." Notably, Richard never accuses himself of anything more than "follies" or occasionally a vague worldliness in contrast to his expectations of eternity. There is no repentance for killing his uncle, disinheriting his cousin, or misruling his kingdom, although Richard seems to acceded to some level of self-knowledge when he reflects that

> Nor I, nor any man that but man is,
> With nothing shall be pleas'd till he be eas'd
> With being nothing.   (5.5.39-41)

Still his bitter resentment of Bolingbroke needs very little to assert itself. However much these prison speeches give us a Richard who imaginatively casts himself in many roles, his dying words assert his kingship, his mystical union with his land and the sacrilegious guilt of his murder: "Exton, thy fierce hand/ Hath with the King's blood stain'd the King's own land." (5.5.109-10).

Shakespeare created a remarkable character in Richard, both guilty and pitiable, both true king and bad king, distasteful in his selfishness and yet sympathetic in his suffering. He may well be the most challenging character before Hamlet for a player to enact on stage, which in turn may be why so many great actors have attempted to do so.

Performance History

Much the most famous performance of *Richard II* occurred on February 7, 1601, the day before the Earl of Essex's unsuccessful rebellion, when a number of his supporters requested that Shakespeare's company, the Lord Chamberlain's Men, stage the play. Unflattering comparisons between Richard II and Queen Elizabeth—largely as monarch disastrously influenced by pernicious and self-seeking advisors—had been fairly frequent for some time. Elizabeth herself famously was quoted as asking "I am Richard II, know you not that?"

But if the playing of *Richard II* was intended to arouse support for Essex, it failed. Londoners refused to rally to him, and he was taken, tried, and executed within three weeks. The players were questioned in the matter, but their claim to have reluctantly accepted a £2 subsidy to perform what they considered an uncommercial old play was apparently accepted, and they suffered no penalty.

The incident is sometimes supposed to have relevance to the curious fact that when *Richard II* had appeared in print for the first time four years earlier in 1596, the text omitted the scene in which Richard actually appears on stage and is deposed—a passage of about 160 lines. The passage was also omitted from the next two editions, the second quarto of 1596 and the third quarto of 1597; it never appeared in print until 1608, four years after Elizabeth's death.

Some form of censorship was operative here: either officially by the authorities like the Archbishop of Canterbury and the Bishop of London; or perhaps more likely, prudent self-censorship by the publisher, who foresaw a potential problem. Most critics, including Kittredge, however, presume that the deposition scene, although excised in print, was regularly performed on stage, where censorship was in the hands of a different authority, the office of the Master of the Revels. One would imagine that what Essex's supporters requested would certainly have included the scene of Richard's fall

As with many Shakespeare plays, *Richard II* during the Restoration and the eighteenth century was almost invariably played in an adapted form. Nahum Tate prepared an adaptation in 1680 and Lewis Theobald another in 1719. In the nineteenth century, *Richard II*, again like many other Shakespeare plays, became a favorite occasion for stage spectacle; perhaps the most extreme example was Charles Kean's 1857 version, which brought 600 persons on stage for Richard and Bolingbroke's return to London—a scene, by the way, that does not occur in Shakespeare.

The most significant change in the play's reputation came fairly early in the twentieth century with acclaimed performances of the title role by John Gielgud in London, in both 1929 and 1937, and by Maurice Evans in New York in 1937. Gielgud, of course, was one of the century's greatest Shakespearean actors, but Evans's reputation is surprising, especially for viewers who remember him as a comic warlock on television or a benevolent chimpanzee in the *Planet of the Apes* films. Both performers demonstrated the breadth and variety of the character as well as the remarkable histrionic talents necessary to fully actuate the role. From this time on, *Richard II* became a role to challenge the resources of the aspiring Shakespearean, not quite as essential as doing a Hamlet, but not too much less impressive.

Richard II on screen

To the best of my knowledge there has never been a theatrically released motion picture of *Richard II*, not even among the hundreds produced in the silent era. There have been however, a number of television versions, four of which will be discussed below.

Unfortunately, some interesting versions are omitted. There is apparently no film or tape record of John Gielgud, the twentieth century's most distinguished Richard, performing the role. There is an existing kinescope of Maurice Evans' 1954 performance for the Hallmark Hall of Fame, but it is available only in archives such as the Folger or the New York Public Library, and not commercially. The English Shakespeare Company did a very notable version of *Richard II* as part of its *Wars of the Roses* series; it starred the talented Michael Pennington and was set, intriguingly, in the Regency period. But the version seems to be available only as part of the complete series, and at a cost of 500 to 600 dollars, much beyond most academic budgets.

The following versions are available at reasonable cost, and the performance notes for this volume were be drawn from the first three of these performances; the last of these versions, it will become clear, is only marginally useful.

1960 *Kings: William Shakespeare's An Age of Kings* was a pioneering series of television plays produced for the BBC by Peter Dews. It presented eight of Shakespeare's histories, from *Richard II* to *Richard III*, in historical order with each play compressed to two episodes of approximately one hour. (*Henry VI, Part 1*, was collapsed into a single episode.) The episodes were shown on a biweekly basis, and were quite successful both in England, and a year later in the United States. Comparatively speaking, *Kings* was subject to a number of limitations: it was shot in black and white—there was no color television in Britain at the time; the time limits required somewhat considerable cutting; and the shows were filmed live, with live performance's potential for mishap. What is remarkable, however, is how the strengths of this version make these limitations seem inconsiderable. The quality of the acting is excellent throughout. Peter Dews had a "resident company" of twenty-two young men, many with experience at the Old Vic, who took on remarkable numbers of supporting roles over the course of the series, as many as ten or eleven in as many as twelve or thirteen episodes. The leading roles were acted by visiting performers, not glamorous stars, but often actors with substantial reputations on the stage. The leading roles of course often continued into the following episodes; for example, Tom Fleming, who here is a peremptory Bolingbroke, will continue as the troubled king in *Henry IV, Parts 1* and 2. A young Sean Connery begins here as Harry Percy (Hotspur to be); this is two years before he became Bond (James Bond). The production is well costumed and mounted, and although the permanent set can at times seem constricting or uncomfortably familiar, there are also times when it allows for a striking setting or transition between settings. The performance text for the entire series was published by Pyramid Books in 1961, and the series has recently become available on DVD at reasonable cost.

1978 *BBC*: This is of course the version of *Richard II* performed as part of "The Shakespeare Plays," the Time-Life supported initiative that over the course of eight years presented television versions of all 36 of the Folio plays, as well as *Pericles*. The series is generally considered a mixed success at best, and the same judgment was made of the six plays of the opening season of 1978, which included the *Richard II* discussed here. The first producer of the series was Cedric Messina, whose intention was to achieve versions of the plays that were "in permanent form, accessible to audiences throughout the world… performed by some of the greatest classical actors of our time." Messina seems to have avoided the adjective "definitive," but at the least he clearly aimed at productions that were traditional in approach, realistic in presentation, and performed in a style validated by previous performance and criticism. At least for *Richard II*, the results justify the overall strategy espoused by Messina and the play's director, David Giles. The great strength of the version is of course the remarkable depth of talent of the cast. Derek Jacobi has the range and variety of resources to embody the shifting moods and fortunes of the King. John Gielgud is, expectedly, an excellent Gaunt and does the famous "royal throne of kings" speech with great effect. Jon Finch, Polanski's Macbeth some seven years earlier, presents both a strong and ambivalent Bolingbroke. Wendy Hiller and Mary Morris, both actresses with exceptionally long and distinguished careers, offer brief but highly effective appearances in minor roles. Charles Gray, the play's York, was universally praised for his strength and coherence in one of the most difficult supporting roles in a Shakespearean history play. Beyond this, *BBC*, with the largest budget and the most mobile camera, makes the visual presentation of its world a frequent substantial strength of the performance. The text of the *BBC* version was published by Mayflower Books in 1978; this edition indicates the cuts in the playing text—287 of 2757 total lines; the relatively light cutting was also part of the series' intention. *Kings* cuts more heavily; *Bard*, quite deliberately, cuts less.

1982 *Bard*: In the early 1980s Bard Productions Ltd. produced as many as nine television versions of Shakespeare plays. As the dates might suggest, the Bard versions were much influenced by the BBC plays, which had begun three years earlier. There was at the time considerable acrimony at the exclusion of American actors from the BBC project, even though the financial support for the project was in great part from American sources. Something of this animosity can be felt in *Bard*'s insistence that the plays as performed by American actors with familiar accents would be much more accessible for American students. Accordingly, the Bard productions tended to feature players who were familiar, at least as faces, to the American television viewer of the 1980s. For *Richard II*, the title role was played by David Birney, who had starred as the male lead on the TV situation comedy *Bridget Loves Bernie*, and his queen was Mary Joan Negro, who had appeared on the soap opera *Another World*. The quality of acting, as might be expected, is professionally competent, although the actors often demonstrate facial expressions or body language or even vocal intonations more suitable for the naturalistic style they usually practiced. Few of the cast exhibit the depth or range of the best of the performers on *Kings* or *BBC*. The *Bard Richard II* displays a good deal more than the general influence of the BBC version. William Woodman, the director, like *BBC*'s David Giles, places a number of the later scenes at night, which the narrative does not seem to invite. Further, Woodman has David Birney in the prison scene read his first line to the Groom, "Thanks, noble peer,/ The cheapest of us is ten groats too dear," lying on his back and keeping his eyes closed while he speaks; since Derek Jacobi had done the same for *BBC*, this hardly seems coincidence. It might also be noted that on viewing the *BBC* and *Bard* versions together, it seems clear that *Bard* commits itself to playing whatever *BBC* omitted, even though *BBC* was formally committed to playing relatively complete texts. A number of the more surprising inclusions are indicated in the notes on performance. The other pedagogical claim that *Bard* frequently made is that they were performing the play "as seen in the Sixteenth Century." The playing area for *Richard II* (referred to as an "Elizabethan stage" in the closing credits) is basically a bare platform stage with a second platform, serving as a sort of equivalent of the gallery or upper stage of the Globe, running the length of the stage; there are also two staircases from the higher to the lower level, usually flanking a center entrance area, but repositioned at various times during the performance. In the opening scenes, the *Bard Richard II* does seem to create something of the sense of an open, undecorated, fluid playing space, much like Shakespeare's Globe. *Bard's* only substantial cut is the scene between Gaunt and the Duchess of Gloucester (Act 1, scene 2), which allows an easy continuity in the playing of Bolingbroke and Mowbray's challenges and then their preparation for the duel. From this point on, however, it is hard to see what advantage the pseudo-Elizabethan staging offers: there are a number of scenes that simply keep the camera closed in on a small part of the set, perhaps the foot of a staircase and a bit of the platform. Even more notably, there are a number of scenes that are played in what is established as a confined, interior space, achieved by setting the action against a rear or side wall, or in a corner between the two, or with a curtain representing a wall of the implied room. Richard's prison cell at Pomfret, with its open ceiling, seems impossible in this staging, but since we are never given a shot that establishes the totality of the playing space, it is hard to be sure. At any rate, the actual filming of the scenes so often leaves the implicit staging of the opening scene that the much advertised setting seems to pay small dividends if any.

2001 (John Farrell) Farrell's independent film of *Richard II* was shot with so little in the way of resources that it seems almost cruel to point out its shortcomings. It is, however, in many ways an amateurish production; this is particularly true of the acting, since no one in the cast appears capable of reading iambic pentameter. The film was shot at Fort Strong, a long-deserted army installation on an island in Boston harbor. This is the only version of *Richard II* that was in fact filmed on location rather than in a studio. The setting provides a number of stone walls and steps, the shells of a few concrete buildings, and a couple of underground passages for Richard's prison cell at Pomfret. The surrounding landscape is heavily overgrown with scrub trees, weeds, and extensive underbrush. There is a general impression of a post-apocalyptic world, contrasted frequently with shots of the waters of the harbor and the sky above them. Farrell has cut at least three-quarters of the text, leaving almost nothing in the language of ceremony or the concern with kingly sanctity usually thought so crucial in *Richard II*. When Northumberland enlists the other lords (a version of Act 2, scene 1), his talk of extravagance, excessive taxation, inherited estates, even nobles and commons, all seem concepts that have no meaning in the impoverished world we are given here. This is virtually a world without possessions: Richard has what looks like a dining room chair for his first appearance; John of Gaunt has a wheelchair and a pipe; Bushy, oddly, a small book of poetry; and this is almost all. Farrell rather heavy-handedly insists that the white cap Richard wears is the equivalent of the crown mentioned so often in the text. When Richard returns from Ireland, one of his soldiers is required to try to balance it on its pillow with one hand while brandishing an Uzi with the other. And during the deposition, Richard extends the cap to Bolingbroke and, quite impishly, drops it on the ground as the other reaches out. All of the actors seem to have only their costumes, which even for the women are bits and pieces of army uniforms, and their weapons. There may be more guns per capita in Farrell's film than in Luhrmann's

Romeo + Juliet, and like the costumes, these are a motley collection of Uzis, AK-47s, M-1 rifles, several varieties of shotgun, automatics, and six shooters. The world of the film's poverty all but precludes interior shots; aside from Richard's prison, no one has any place to be except outdoors. The question of what is being competed for thus awkwardly poses itself.

What Farrell's film does have in abundance is violence, in spite of the fact that it is customary to note how little violence there is in *Richard II*. Farrell, however, takes whatever the text suggests as having a potentiality for violence, actuates it, and often exaggerates it. For example, the duel between Bolingbroke and Mowbray does take place, at least to the extent of having them roll around on the ground, wrestling for a wicked-looking knife, until Richard stops the fight with a burst of machine-gun fire. The capture of Bushy and Green, implicit in Bolingbroke's judgment of them in Act 3, scene 1, is here played out as a full-fledged combat (the battle of Bushy Green?). Farrell uses what little he has available as special effects, with some explosions, smoke, much running, pointing weapons and falling down dead. Farrell seems to have cut into his footage some clips obtained elsewhere; there is a shot of men running that seems not to be Farrell's because they are uniformly dressed in t-shirts and fatigue pants and are unarmed. Richard's death is of course also much extended. He steals a pistol and kills two of the intended murderers in his cell, bursts out of an underground tunnel to shoot two more, hunts down Willoughby and cuts his throat, and also has Ross (whom the film unites with Exton) with knife to his throat when he changes his mind. Richard leaves the disarmed Ross, and runs downhill to the water; but another of Ross's men appears with an AK-47, butt-stokes the Ross who tries to impede him, and shoots Richard a total of four times. Richard dies at the water's edge, as the sun sinks symbolically below the horizon, and the tide, equally symbolically, washes over his body.

Beyond this, Farrell manages to provide yet further violence by creating new episodes. When Richard returns from Ireland, the faithful Aumerle (a woman in this version) spots a couple of scouts on a nearby bluff, hunts them down, stabs one, and shoots the other. The Queen, after learning of the impending deposition—her lady in waiting has to be restrained from spraying the Gardener with her Uzi—is being escorted, presumably to Richard, by four soldiers. They are ambushed and wiped out by Bolingbroke's men, and after some moments of hiding and seeking, the lead ambusher captures the Queen. She has her farewell scene (a version of Act 5, scene 1) with Richard, but escapes from Northumberland, who seems to be conducting her to deportation to France; she does so by pushing him to his death off a rampart, and then disables Northumberland's guard by seizing his genitals. This allows her to steal back to Richard's prison, where, in an incoherent sequence, she says she is the devoted groom of the text, and Richard does not recognize her. The Keeper's "Fellow, give place. Here is no longer stay" becomes the Queen's recapture, and while Richard is escaping, the sharpshooter who will eventually kill him stabs the Queen in the back. Richard returns, and before resuming combat, spends about a minute and a half of mute screen time caressing her face. The fact that so many of the killers and the killed are anonymous combatants who appear nowhere else—the scouts, the escorts, the ambushers, the would-be regicides, the sharpshooter, Northumberland's guard—makes the case very strongly that the only thing that seems to be at stake among the people of Farrell's film is catching and killing one another. Since Farrell's special effects budget apparently did not allow for blood pellets—given the number of deaths, this is an amazingly unsanguinary film—or for bullets whizzing and ricocheting off the walls, the violence works out to pointing a gun at someone, a gunshot on the sound track, and the antagonist falling down, agonized death cry optional. This is uncomfortably close to what children do when "playing guns," except that the victims are somewhat more cooperative. It is even closer, considering the contemporary uniforms and weapons and the overgrown landscape, to what week-end enthusiasts of the pastime call "paint ball."

—Thomas A. Pendleton
2012

THE TRAGEDY OF
KING RICHARD THE SECOND

Dramatis Personæ.

King Richard II.
John of Gaunt, Duke of Lancaster, ⎫
Edmund of Langley, Duke of York, ⎭   uncles to the King.
Henry, surnamed *Bolingbroke,* Duke of Hereford,
    son to *John of Gaunt;* afterwards *King Henry IV.*
Duke of Aumerle, son to the *Duke of York.*
Thomas Mowbray, Duke of Norfolk.
Duke of Surrey.
Earl of Salisbury.
Lord Berkeley.
Bushy, ⎫
Bagot, ⎬   servants to King Richard.
Green, ⎭
Earl of Northumberland.
Henry Percy, surnamed *Hotspur,* his son.
Lord Ross.
Lord Willoughby.
Lord Fitzwater.
Bishop of Carlisle.
Abbot of Westminster.
Lord Marshal.
Sir Stephen Scroop.
Sir Pierce of Exton.
Captain of a band of Welshmen.
Two Gardeners.

Queen to King Richard.
Duchess of York.
Duchess of Gloucester.
Ladies attending on the Queen.

Lords, Heralds, Officers, Soldiers, Keeper, Messenger, Groom, and other Attendants.

Scene. — England and Wales.

1

ACT I

Scene I. [*London. The Palace.*]

Enter King Richard, John of Gaunt, with other Nobles and Attendants.[†]

KING   Old John of Gaunt, time-honored Lancaster,
Hast thou, according to thy oath and band,
Brought hither Henry Hereford, thy bold son,
Here to make good the boist'rous late appeal,
Which then our leisure would not let us hear,   5
Against the Duke of Norfolk, Thomas Mowbray?

GAUNT   I have, my liege.

KING   Tell me, moreover, hast thou sounded him
If he appeal the Duke on ancient malice,
Or worthily, as a good subject should,   10
On some known ground of treachery in him?

GAUNT   As near as I could sift him on that argument,
On some apparent danger seen in him
Aim'd at your Highness, no inveterate malice.

KING   Then call them to our presence.   [*Exit Attendant.*]
Face to face,   15
And frowning brow to brow, ourselves will hear
The accuser and the accused freely speak.
High-stomach'd are they both and full of ire,
In rage deaf as the sea, hasty as fire.

Enter Bolingbroke and Mowbray.

BOLINGBROKE   Many years of happy days befall   20
My gracious sovereign, my most loving liege!

ACT I. SCENE I.
1–4. **John of Gaunt:** So called from his birthplace, Gaunt (Ghent) in Flanders. He was fifty-eight years old at this time. —**band:** bond. —**Hereford:** Duke of Hereford. —**appeal:** accusation. 5. **our...us:** The so-called "royal *we*" The King is speaking officially. 9–10. **appeal:** accuse. —**on ancient malice:** because of some old grudge. —**worthily:** deservedly. 12–13. **As near...argument:** as closely as I could examine him on that subject. —**apparent:** manifest. 16. **ourselves:** oneself; I, the king in person. 18. **High-stomach'd:** haughty (T.P.).

[†]   In spite of the quarrel, the scene presents what ought to be an ideal setting for the relevant relationships: the King on his throne, dispensing justice and his subjects, standing or kneeling before him, acknowledging his authority and protesting their loyalty. *BBC* presents the most sumptuous setting with a spacious royal chamber and a throne atop three steps. *Bard*, a little limited by the stage setting, is similar, if somewhat less impressive. *Kings* has Richard seated at a table, with Mowbray and Bolingbroke at the end of the table only three feet or so away; the effect is a little claustrophobic.

King Richard (David Birney) hears the accusations of Bolingbrook (Paul Shenat), left, and Mowbray (Jeff Pomerantz). The favorites flanking the King are left to right, Green (William Gamble), Bagot (Michael Cummings), Bushy (Jay T. Loudenback), and Aumerle (DeVeren Bookwalter). (*Bard*, 1981)

MOWBRY	Each day still better other's happiness Until the heavens, envying earth's good hap, Add an immortal title to your crown!
KING	We thank you both. Yet one but flatters us, As well appeareth by the cause you come— Namely, to appeal each other of high treason. Cousin of Hereford, what dost thou object Against the Duke of Norfolk, Thomas Mowbray?
BOLINGBROKE	First—heaven be the record to my speech!— In the devotion of a subject's love, Tend'ring the precious safety of my prince And free from other misbegotten hate, Come I appellant to this princely presence.

25

30

---

24. **Add an immortal title to your crown!:** "make you a king in heaven." 25. **We, us:** The "royal *we*." 26. **As...the cause you come:** as is made evident by the reason for which you thus put in an appearance before us. 28. **what dost thou object?:** What is the charge that you bring? 30. **heaven be the record to my speech:** I call upon God to bear witness to what I say 32. **Tend'ring:** out of regard for. 33. **free... hate:** free from any hatred except that which I feel for treason 34. **appellant:** The technical term for the accuser. Mowbray is the *defendant*.

Now, Thomas Mowbray, do I turn to thee,   35
And mark my greeting well; for what I speak
My body shall make good upon this earth
Or my divine soul answer it in heaven.
Thou art a traitor and a miscreant,
Too good to be so, and too bad to live,   40
Since the more fair and crystal is the sky,
The uglier seem the clouds that in it fly.
Once more, the more to aggravate the note,
With a foul traitor's name stuff I thy throat
And wish (so please my sovereign), ere I move,   45
What my tongue speaks my right-drawn sword may prove.

MOWBRY   Let not my cold words here accuse my zeal.
'Tis not the trial of a woman's war,
The bitter clamor of two eager tongues,
Can arbitrate this cause betwixt us twain;   50
The blood is hot that must be cool'd for this.
Yet can I not of such tame patience boast
As to be hush'd and naught at all to say.
First, the fair reverence of your Highness curbs me
From giving reins and spurs to my free speech,   55
Which else would post until it had return'd
These terms of treason doubled down his throat.
Setting aside his high blood's royalty,
And let him be no kinsman to my liege,
I do defy him and I spit at him,   60
Call him a slanderous coward and a villain;
Which to maintain, I would allow him odds
And meet him, were I tied to run afoot
Even to the frozen ridges of the Alps,
Or any other ground inhabitable   65
Where ever Englishman durst set his foot.

36–40. **what I speak…heaven:** I will prove my accusation by wager of battle here upon earth, or, if I fall, my immortal soul shall answer for the truth of it before the bar of divine justice. 39. **a miscreant:** a faithless man. 40. **Too good:** too high in rank. 43. **to aggravate the note:** to make the disgrace the heavier by reiteration. *Note* here has the sense of "stigma," "brand of infamy." 45. **so please:** so may it please; if it please. —**move:** leave my station of defiance. 46. **right-drawn:** drawn in a right or just cause. 47. **Let not my cold words here accuse my zeal:** Though I speak without passion, let not my calm words cast doubt upon the intensity of my feelings. 48. **the trial of a woman's war:** the test afforded by a contest in scolding. 49. **eager:** sharp, shrewish 50. **Can:** that can. 51. **cool'd:** i.e., by the death of one of us the combatants. 54. **the fair reverence of your Highness:** the reverence that is due to your Majesty. 56. **post:** ride at high speed—posthaste . 58–59. **Setting…royalty…liege:** disregarding the fact that he is of royal blood, and treating him as if he were not your Majesty's kinsman. 63. **tied:** required (by the terms of the combat). 64. **inhabitable:** uninhabitable.

Meantime let this defend my loyalty—
By all my hopes, most falsely doth he lie.

BOLINGBROKE Pale trembling coward, there I throw my gage,
Disclaiming here the kinred of the King,   70
And lay aside my high blood's royalty,
Which fear, not reverence, makes thee to except.
If guilty dread have left thee so much strength
As to take up mine honor's pawn, then stoop.
By that and all the rites of knighthood else,   75
Will I make good against thee, arm to arm,
What I have spoke or thou canst worse devise.

MOWBRY   I take it up; and by that sword I swear
Which gently laid my knighthood on my shoulder,
I'll answer thee in any fair degree   80
Or chivalrous design of knightly trial;
And when I mount, alive may I not light
If I be traitor or unjustly fight!

KING   What doth our cousin lay to Mowbray's charge?
It must be great that can inherit us   85
So much as of a thought of ill in him.

BOLINGBROKE Look, what I speak, my life shall prove it true—
That Mowbray hath receiv'd eight thousand nobles
In name of lendings for your Highness' soldiers,
The which he hath detain'd for lewd employments,   90
Like a false traitor and injurious villain.
Besides I say, and will in battle prove—
Or here, or elsewhere to the furthest verge
That ever was survey'd by English eye—
That all the treasons for these eighteen years   95
Complotted and contrived in this land
Fetch from false Mowbray their first head and spring.

---

67. **this:** Emphatic: "this one sentence—'he lies.'" 69. **By all my hopes:** An oath: "I swear by all that I have to hope for, whether in this world or the next." 69. **my gage:** my pledge of defiance. Doubtless a glove. 70. **Disclaiming here the kinred of the King:** renouncing all claim to any privilege that my kinship to the King may confer. 72. **fear, not reverence:** Bolingbroke declares that Mowbray's exception was due to fear of *him*, not to reverence for the King or for royal blood. 77. **or thou canst worse devise:** or any other worse accusation against you that you can imagine me as making. 78. **by that sword:** Mowbray swears by the King's sword which had dubbed him knight. 80–81. **I'll answer thee...knightly trial:** I accept your challenge and I will meet you in any form of combat that accords with the rules of chivalry 82. **light:** alight, dismount. 85–86. **inherit us So much as of a thought:** make me entertain even a thought. 88. **nobles:** gold coins worth one third of a pound sterling. 89. **lendings:** money advanced to soldiers when the regular pay cannot be given. 90. **for lewd employments:** for his own ignoble purposes. 93. **verge:** boundary. 97. **head:** source.

Further I say, and further will maintain
Upon his bad life to make all this good,
That he did plot the Duke of Gloucester's death,†   100
Suggest his soon-believing adversaries,
And consequently, like a traitor coward,
Sluic'd out his innocent soul through streams of blood;
Which blood, like sacrificing Abel's, cries,
Even from the tongueless caverns of the earth,   105
To me for justice and rough chastisement;
And, by the glorious worth of my descent,
This arm shall do it, or this life be spent.

KING   How high a pitch his resolution soars!
                Thomas of Norfolk, what say'st thou to this?   110

MOWBRY   O, let my sovereign turn away his face
                And bid his ears a little while be deaf,
                Till I have told this slander of his blood
                How God and good men hate so foul a liar!

KING   Mowbray, impartial are our eyes and ears.   115
                Were he my brother, nay, my kingdom's heir,
                As he is but my father's brother's son,
                Now by my sceptre's awe I make a vow,
                Such neighbour nearness to our sacred blood
                Should nothing privilege him nor partialize   120
                The unstooping firmness of my upright soul.
                He is our subject, Mowbray; so art thou:
                Free speech and fearless I to thee allow.

MOWBRY   Then, Bolingbroke, as low as to thy heart
                Through the false passage of thy throat, thou liest!   125

98–99. **will maintain...good:** will undertake to prove all this in a combat that shall put an end to his evil life. 100. **the Duke of Gloucester's death:** Thomas of Woodstock, the seventh son of Edward III, was accused of treason and put to death (or murdered) in 1397. 101–103. **Suggest his soon-believing adversaries:** did induce the Duke's credulous enemies to believe him guilty of treason. —**consequently:** in pursuance of that course of villainy. 107. **worth:** honor. —**my descent:** i.e., from Edward III. 109. **How high a pitch his resolution soars!:** A *pitch* is the highest point reached by a soaring falcon. 113. **this slander of his blood:** this man who is a disgrace to the King's ancestral line. 118. **my scepter's awe:** the reverence due to my scepter. 120. **nothing:** not at all. —**partialize:** make partial in judgment. 125. **thy throat:** "Thou liest in thy throat!" is an old insulting form of expressing the contrast with a merely casual falsehood—a lie with the *lips*. Mowbray, however, declares that Bolingbroke's lie comes from his false *heart*.

---

†   Since it will be established that Richard himself is ultimately responsible for Gloucester's death, all three versions move to a close-up—a very natural tactic for the medium. Jacobi in *BBC* and Birney in *Bard* manage to retain their composure with only a little difficulty. *Kings* does a fast zoom to an extreme close-up of David William, the camera movement more than the facial expression suggesting a guilty reaction.

Three parts of that receipt I had for Calais
Disburs'd I duly to his Highness' soldiers.
The other part reserv'd I by consent.
For that my sovereign liege was in my debt
Upon remainder of a dear account   130
Since last I went to France to fetch his queen.
Now swallow down that lie! For Gloucester's death,
I slew him not, but, to my own disgrace,
Neglected my sworn duty in that case.
For you, my noble Lord of Lancaster,   135
The honorable father to my foe,
Once did I lay an ambush for your life—
A trespass that doth vex my grieved soul;
But ere I last receiv'd the sacrament,
I did confess it and exactly begg'd   140
Your Grace's pardon, and I hope I had it.
This is my fault. As for the rest appeal'd,
It issues from the rancour of a villain,
A recreant and most degenerate traitor;
Which in myself I boldly will defend,   145
And interchangeably hurl down my gage
Upon this overweening traitor's foot
To prove myself a loyal gentleman
Even in the best blood chamber'd in his bosom.
In haste whereof most heartily I pray   150
Your Highness to assign our trial day.

KING   Wrath-kindled gentlemen, be rul'd by me;
Let's purge this choler without letting blood.
This we prescribe, though no physician;
Deep malice makes too deep incision.   155
Forget, forgive; conclude and be agreed;

---

126. **that receipt I had for Calais:** that sum that I received as payment for the garrison at Calais.
—**Three parts:** Three quarters. [T.P.] 129. **For that:** because. 130-31. **Upon remainder...account...
France:** on account toward the payment of the balance due me on a heavy debt that had been incurred
when I went to France the last time. 132–33. **For:** as for. —**I slew him not, etc.:** Bolingbroke has seemed
to accuse Mowbray of killing the Duke of Gloucester with his own hands. Mowbray alleges, on the
contrary, that it was his "sworn duty," as Deputy of Calais, to have the Duke executed as a traitor, but that
he had been remiss in the performance of that duty. 140. **exactly:** specifically 142. **the rest appeal'd:** the
rest of the charges brought against me by Bolingbroke. 144. **recreant:** false to his allegiance. A *recreant*
is, literally, "one who renounces his faith." 145. **Which...defend:** And this assertion I will maintain in
person in my defence. 146. **interchangeably:** in acceptance of the challenge—literally, "mutually." 149
chamber'd: enclosed. [T.P.] 150. **In haste whereof:** and in order to bring this proof to an immediate
demonstration. 153. **Let's purge this choler...blood:** A medical figure. *Choler* means (1) "bile" and (2)
"anger." Wrath was sometimes ascribed to an excess of bile in the system. For a bilious attack the proper
remedy would be to take a purgative (a cleansing medicine) rather than to be bled. 155. **malice:** enmity.

        Our doctors say this is no month to bleed.
        Good uncle, let this end where it begun;
        We'll calm the Duke of Norfolk, you your son.

GAUNT   To be a make-peace shall become my age.   160
        Throw down, my son, the Duke of Norfolk's gage.

KING   And, Norfolk, throw down his.

GAUNT   When, Harry? When?
        Obedience bids I should not bid again.

KING   Norfolk, throw down, we bid. There is no boot.

MOWBRY   Myself I throw, dread sovereign, at thy foot.   165
        My life thou shalt command, but not my shame.
        The one my duty owes; but my fair name,
        Despite of death that lives upon my grave,
        To dark dishonour's use thou shalt not have.
        I am disgrac'd, impeach'd, and baffled here;   170
        Pierc'd to the soul with slander's venom'd spear,
        The which no balm can cure but his heartblood
        Which breath'd this poison.

KING   Rage must be withstood.
        Give me his gage. Lions make leopards tame.

MOWBRY   Yea, but not change his spots! Take but my shame,   175
        And I resign my gage. My dear dear lord,
        The purest treasure mortal times afford
        Is spotless reputation. That away,
        Men are but gilded loam or painted clay.
        A jewel in a ten times barr'd-up chest   180
        Is a bold spirit in a loyal breast.
        Mine honour is my life. Both grow in one;
        Take honour from me, and my life is done.
        Then, dear my liege, mine honor let me try;
        In that I live, and for that will I die.   185

KING   Cousin, throw up your gage. Do you begin.

BOLINGBROKE O, God defend my soul from such deep sin!

---

160. **a makepeace:** a peacemaker. 162. **When, Harry? when?:** *When* is common as an interjection of insistent or impatient command. 164. **There is no boot:** There's no help for it—i.e., You must obey orders. 168. **Despite of death that lives upon my grave:** which will live (in my epitaph) upon my grave after I am dead. 170. **impeach'd:** formally accused of heinous crimes. —**baffled:** To *baffle* is, literally, to "degrade from knighthood." 173. **Which:** who. —**breath'd:** uttered. 177. **mortal times:** our life on this earth. 184. **dear my liege:** *My lord* and similar titles are often treated as compound words and limited by an adjective. —**try:** i.e., by combat; by wager of battle. 186. **throw up your gage:** toss up and away the Duke's glove that you are holding.

Shall I seem crestfallen in my father's sight?
Or with pale beggar-fear impeach my height
Before this outdar'd dastard? Ere my tongue   190
Shall wound my honor with such feeble wrong
Or sound so base a parle, my teeth shall tear
The slavish motive of recanting fear
And spit it bleeding in his high disgrace,
Where shame doth harbor, even in Mowbray's face. *Exit Gaunt.* 195

KING   We were not born to sue, but to command;
Which since we cannot do to make you friends,
Be ready, as your lives shall answer it,
At Coventry upon Saint Lambert's day.
There shall your swords and lances arbitrate   200
The swelling difference of your settled hate:
Since we cannot atone you, we shall see
Justice design the victor's chivalry.
Lord Marshal, command our officers-at-arms
Be ready to direct these home alarms.   *Exeunt.* 205

Scene II. [*London. The Duke of Lancaster's Palace.*]

Enter John of Gaunt with the Duchess of Gloucester.†

GAUNT   Alas, the part I had in Woodstock's blood
Doth more solicit me than your exclaims
To stir against the butchers of his life!
But since correction lieth in those hands
Which made the fault that we cannot correct,   5
Put we our quarrel to the will of heaven,
Who, when they see the hours ripe on earth,
Will rain hot vengeance on offenders' heads.

---

189. **impeach my height:** discredit my lofty rank 190. **outdar'd:** cowed. 191. **with such feeble wrong:** by insulting it by such a false confession of cowardice. 192. **sound so base a parle:** give notice of my willingness to negotiate for peace when peace would be so shameful. 193. **slavish motive:** dishonorable instrument or organ, i.e., his tongue. 199. **Saint Lambert's day:** September 17th. 202–203. **atone:** reconcile. —**we shall see Justice design the victor's chivalry:** we shall see justice determine whose knightly prowess shall win the victory.

Act I. scene II.
1. **the part I had in Woodstock's blood:** my relationship to Woodstock. Thomas of Woodstock, Duke of Gloucester, was John of Gaunt's brother. 4–6. **those hands:** i.e., the King's hands. "Only the King can punish the murderer, and it was the King himself who procured the murder.". —**made:** committed. —**our quarrel:** our cause. 7. **they:** *Heaven* is often used as a plural.

† *Kings* and *Bard*, like many stage productions, cut the scene. *BBC*, however, gives us firmly Richard's responsibility for Gloucester's murder. It also introduces the first of the play's three noblewomen, each of whom is virtually defined by her menfolk's misfortunes.

DUCHESS	Finds brotherhood in thee no sharper spur?
	Hath love in thy old blood no living fire?	10
	Edward's seven sons, whereof thyself art one,
	Were as seven vials of his sacred blood,
	Or seven fair branches springing from one root.
	Some of those seven are dried by nature's course,
	Some of those branches by the Destinies cut;	15
	But Thomas, my dear lord, my life, my Gloucester,
	One vial full of Edward's sacred blood,
	One flourishing branch of his most royal root,
	Is crack'd, and all the precious liquor spilt,
	Is hack'd down, and his summer leaves all faded,	20
	By envy's hand and murder's bloody axe.
	Ah, Gaunt, his blood was thine! That bed, that womb,
	That metal, that self mould that fashioned thee,
	Made him a man; and though thou livest and breathest,
	Yet art thou slain in him. Thou dost consent	25
	In some large measure to thy father's death
	In that thou seest thy wretched brother die,
	Who was the model of thy father's life.
	Call it not patience, Gaunt; it is despair.
	In suff'ring thus thy brother to be slaught'red	30
	Thou showest the naked pathway to thy life,
	Teaching stern murder how to butcher thee.
	That which in mean men we entitle patience
	Is pale cold cowardice in noble breasts.
	What shall I say? To safeguard thine own life	35
	The best way is to venge my Gloucester's death.
GAUNT	God's is the quarrel; for God's substitute,
	His deputy anointed in his sight,
	Hath caus'd his death; the which if wrongfully,
	Let heaven revenge; for I may never lift	40
	An angry arm against his minister.
DUCHESS	Where then, alas, may I complain myself?
GAUNT	To God, the widow's champion and defence.
DUCHESS	Why then, I will. Farewell, old Gaunt.

21. **envy's:** *Envy* has the general sense of "malicious enmity"—not the special sense to which it is limited in modern usage. 23. **metal:** substance, material. —**self:** selfsame. 25. **dost consent:** acquiesce [T.P.] 27. **In that:** inasmuch as. 28. **thy model of the father's life:** a copy (the image) of your father; 29. **patience:** self-control. 31. **naked:** defenceless; open to any assailant. 33. **mean:** of low degree; of humble station. 37. **God's substitute:** the King. 38. **anointed:** Anointing with holy oil was a part of the ceremony of coronation. 41. **his minister:** God's agent upon earth—practically synonymous with *substitute* and *deputy.* 42. **may:** can.

Thou goest to Coventry, there to behold   45
Our cousin Hereford and fell Mowbray fight.
O, sit my husband's wrongs on Hereford's spear,
That it may enter butcher Mowbray's breast!
Or, if misfortune miss the first career,
Be Mowbray's sins so heavy in his bosom   50
That they may break his foaming courser's back
And throw the rider headlong in the lists,
A caitiff recreant to my cousin Hereford!
Farewell, old Gaunt. Thy sometimes brother's wife
With her companion, Grief, must end her life.   55

GAUNT   Sister, farewell; I must to Coventry.
As much good stay with thee as go with me!

DUCHESS   Yet one word more! Grief boundeth where it falls,
Not with the empty hollowness, but weight.
I take my leave before I have begun,   60
For sorrow ends not when it seemeth done.
Commend me to thy brother, Edmund York.
Lo, this is all. Nay, yet depart not so!
Though this be all, do not so quickly go.
I shall remember more. Bid him—ah, what?—
With all good speed at Plashy visit me.   65
Alack, and what shall good old York there see
But empty lodgings and unfurnish'd walls,
Unpeopled offices, untrodden stones?
And what hear there for welcome but my groans?
Therefore commend me—let him not come there   70
To seek out sorrow that dwells everywhere.
Desolate, desolate will I hence and die!
The last leave of thee takes my weeping eye.   *Exeunt.*

---

46. **cousin:** nephew. *Cousin* was used in a general sense—for uncle or aunt, nephew or niece, as well as for cousin in the limited sense. —**fell:** fierce. 47. **sit:** "Let the wrongs sit" [T.P.]. 49. **the first career:** the first course (on horseback) in the combat. 52 **lists:** the arena for jousting 53. **a caitiff recreant to my cousin Hereford:** a miserable vanquished man, whose defeat proves his guilt 54–55. **Thy sometimes brother's wife:** she who was formerly thy brother's wife but is now his widow. —**With...life:** for only death can put an end to her sorrow. 56. **must to:** must go to. 58. **boundeth:** like a ball. 60. **before I have begun:** since I have hardly begun my laments. 65. **Plashy:** the Duke of Gloucester's country residence. 67–68. **unfurnish'd:** stripped of the arras (tapestry hangings) with which the walls of the apartments would be covered when the castle was occupied. —**offices:** the rooms in which domestic servants do their work—kitchen, pantry, etc.

Scene III. [*The lists at Coventry.*]

Enter Lord Marshal and the Duke Aumerle.

MARSHAL   My Lord Aumerle, is Harry Hereford arm'd?

AUMERLE   Yea, at all points, and longs to enter in.

MARSHAL   The Duke of Norfolk, sprightfully and bold,
            Stays but the summons of the appellant's trumpet.

AUMERLE   Why, then the champions are prepar'd, and stay   5
            For nothing but his Majesty's approach.†

*The trumpets sound and the King enters with his Nobles, Gaunt, Bushy, Bagot, Green,
and others. When they are set, enter Mowbray the Duke of Norfolk in arms, defendant,
and Herald.*

KING   Marshal, demand of yonder champion
            The cause of his arrival here in arms.
            Ask him his name and orderly proceed
            To swear him in the justice of his cause.   10

MARSHAL   In God's name and the King's, say who thou art,
            And why thou comest thus knightly clad in arms;
            Against what man thou com'st, and what thy quarrel.
            Speak truly on thy knighthood and thy oath,
            As so defend thee heaven and thy valor!   15

MOWBRY   My name is Thomas Mowbray, Duke of Norfolk,
            Who hither come engaged by my oath
            (Which God defend a knight should violate!)
            Both to defend my loyalty and truth
            To God, my King, and his succeeding issue   20
            Against the Duke of Hereford that appeals me;
            And, by the grace of God and this mine arm,
            To prove him, in defending of myself,
            A traitor to my God, my King, and me;
            And as I truly fight, defend me heaven!   25

ACT I. SCENE III.
2. **to enter in:** into the lists—the barriers enclosing the course where the champions were to meet in battle. 4. **appellant's:** accuser's. 7. **demand:** ask—not in the peremptory modern sense. 9. **orderly:** in due order; in accordance with the rules and regulations for a wager of battle. 10. **swear him:** have him swear to [T.P.]. 13. **thy quarrel:** the cause for which you appear. 17–18. **engaged:** pledged. —**defend:** forbid. 21. **appeals:** accuses. 25. **truly:** in a just cause.

†   All versions give us a highly ceremonial scene, dominated, as in 1.1, by the King on his throne. *BBC*, with the largest resources, is the most sumptuous, including glimpses of Mowbray and Bolingbroke on their warhorses before Richard stops the duel.

The trumpets sound. Enter [Bolingbroke], Duke of Hereford, appellant, in armor, and Herald.

KING Marshal, ask yonder knight in arms
Both who he is and why he cometh hither
Thus plated in habiliments of war;
And formally, according to our law,
Depose him in the justice of his cause. 30

MARSHAL What is thy name? and wherefore com'st thou hither,
Before King Richard in his royal lists?
Against whom comest thou? and what's thy quarrel?
Speak like a true knight, so defend thee heaven!

BOLINGBROKE Harry of Hereford, Lancaster, and Derby 35
Am I, who ready here do stand in arms
To prove, by God's grace and my body's valor
In lists on Thomas Mowbray, Duke of Norfolk,
That he is a traitor, foul and dangerous,
To God of heaven, King Richard, and to me; 40
And as I truly fight, defend me heaven!

MARSHAL On pain of death, no person be so bold
Or daring-hardy as to touch the lists,
Except the Marshal and such officers
Appointed to direct these fair designs. 45

BOLINGBROKE Lord Marshal, let me kiss my sovereign's hand
And bow my knee before his Majesty;
For Mowbray and myself are like two men
That vow a long and weary pilgrimage.
Then let us take a ceremonious leave 50
And loving farewell of our several friends.

MARSHAL The appellant in all duty greets your Highness
And craves to kiss your hand and take his leave.

KING We will descend and fold him in our arms.
Cousin of Hereford, as thy cause is right, 55
So be thy fortune in this royal fight!
Farewell, my blood; which if today thou shed,
Lament we may, but not revenge thee dead.

BOLINGBROKE O, let no noble eye profane a tear
For me, if I be gor'd with Mowbray's spear. 60

---

28. **plated:** in armor of plate. 30. **Depose him:** Take his oath. 45. **these fair designs:** these just and orderly proceedings. 57. **my blood:** metaphorically, my kinsman (T.P.). 59–60. **profane a tear, …:** if I am slain by Mowbray, let no nobleman shed a tear for me.

As confident as is the falcon's flight
Against a bird, do I with Mowbray fight.
My loving lord, I take my leave of you;
Of you, my noble cousin, Lord Aumerle;
Not sick, although I have to do with death,   65
But lusty, young, and cheerly drawing breath.
Lo, as at English feasts, so I regreet
The daintiest last, to make the end most sweet.
O thou, the earthly author of my blood,
Whose youthful spirit, in me regenerate,   70
Doth with a twofold vigor lift me up
To reach at victory above my head,
Add proof unto mine armor with thy prayers,
And with thy blessings steel my lance's point,
That it may enter Mowbray's waxen coat   75
And furbish new the name of John o' Gaunt
Even in the lusty haviour of his son.

GAUNT   God in thy good cause make thee prosperous!
Be swift like lightning in the execution
And let thy blows, doubly redoubled,   80
Fall like amazing thunder on the casque
Of thy adverse pernicious enemy.
Rouse up thy youthful blood; be valiant and live.

BOLINGBROKE Mine innocency and Saint George to thrive!

MOWBRY   However God or fortune cast my lot,   85
There lives or dies, true to King Richard's throne,
A loyal, just, and upright gentleman.
Never did captive with a freer heart
Cast off his chains of bondage and embrace
His golden uncontroll'd enfranchisement,   90
More than my dancing soul doth celebrate
This feast of battle with mine adversary.
Most mighty liege, and my companion peers,
Take from my mouth the wish of happy years.
As gentle and as jocund as to jest   95

---

66. **lusty:** vigorous 67. **regreet:** salute. 68. **daintiest:** finest, tastiest sweets at the end of a banquet [T.P.]. 70. **regenerate:** coming to life again. 71. **two-fold:** i.e., not only with my own natural strength but also with that which you had when you were young. 73. **proof:** strength to resist weapons. A regular term with reference to armor. 75. **waxen:** soft as wax in its defense against my lance's point. 76–77. **furbish new:** add fresh glory to. —**the lusty havior:** brave and vigorous action [T.P.]. 81. **amazing:** *Amaze* was a very strong verb, almost equivalent to "stun" or "paralyze." 81. **casque:** helmet. 85. **cast:** determine. 88. **freer:** more joyful—literally, more free from care. 90. **uncontroll'd enfranchisement:** that liberation which sets him free from captivity. 92. **This feast of battle:** this battle, which is as welcome to me as a festival—a *fête*. 95. **gentle:** calm in mind.

	Go I to fight. Truth hath a quiet breast.
KING	Farewell, my lord. Securely I espy Virtue with valor couched in thine eye. Order the trial, Marshal, and begin.

MARSHAL   Harry of Hereford, Lancaster, and Derby,   100
Receive thy lance, and God defend the right!

BOLINGBROKE   Strong as a tower in hope, I cry amen.

MARSHAL   [*to an Officer*] Go bear this lance to Thomas, Duke of Norfolk.

1. HERALD   Harry of Hereford, Lancaster, and Derby
Stands here for God, his sovereign, and himself,   105
On pain to be found false and recreant,
To prove the Duke of Norfolk, Thomas Mowbray,
A traitor to his God, his King, and him,
And dares him to set forward to the fight.

2. HERALD   Here standeth Thomas Mowbray, Duke of Norfolk,   110
On pain to be found false and recreant,
Both to defend himself and to approve
Henry of Hereford, Lancaster, and Derby
To God, his sovereign, and to him disloyal,
Courageously and with a free desire   115
Attending but the signal to begin.

MARSHAL   Sound trumpets, and set forward combatants. *A charge sounded.*
Stay! The King hath thrown his warder down.

KING   Let them lay by their helmets and their spears
And both return back to their chairs again.   120
Withdraw with us; and let the trumpets sound
While we return these dukes what we decree.   *A long flourish.*
Draw near,

---

112. **to approve:** to prove. 116. **Attending:** awaiting. 118. **his warder:** his staff or truncheon (which he carried as supreme judge of the combat). 121. **Withdraw with us:** with me. Addressed to the members of the King's council. 122. **While...decree:** until I announce to these dukes my decision. —S.D. *flourish:* This flourish of trumpets fills the interval until the King summons the combatants (line 123) to hear the decree.

And list what with our Council we have done.[†]
For that our kingdom's earth should not be soil'd   125
With that dear blood which it hath fostered;
And for our eyes do hate the dire aspect
Of civil wounds plough'd up with neighbours' sword;
And for we think the eagle-winged pride
Of sky-aspiring and ambitious thoughts   130
With rival-hating envy set on you
To wake our peace, which in our country's cradle
Draws the sweet infant breath of gentle sleep;
Which so rous'd up with boist'rous untun'd drums,
With harsh resounding trumpets' dreadful bray   135
And grating shock of wrathful iron arms,
Might from our quiet confines fright fair peace
And make us wade even in our kinred's blood:
Therefore we banish you our territories.
You, cousin Hereford, upon pain of life,   140
Till twice five summers have enrich'd our fields
Shall not regreet our fair dominions
But tread the stranger paths of banishment.

BOLINGBROKE   Your will be done. This must my comfort be—
That sun that warms you here shall shine on me,   145
And those his golden beams to you here lent
Shall point on me and gild my banishment.

KING   Norfolk, for thee remains a heavier doom,
Which I with some unwillingness pronounce:
The sly-slow hours shall not determinate   150
The dateless limit of thy dear exile.

---

124. **list:** listen to. 125. **For that:** in order that. 127. **for:** because. 131. **envy:** enmity. —**set on you:** set you on. 132, **wake:** disturb. 138. **kinred's:** kindred's. 140. **upon pain of life:** with loss of life as the penalty if you disobey. 142. **regreet:** return to—literally, "salute again." 143. **tread …banishment:** wander as an exile in foreign lands. The noun *stranger* is used as an adjective: "alien.." 150–51. **sly-slow:** creeping so slowly along that their passage is almost imperceptible. —**determinate:** bring to an end. —**dateless:** undated—and hence, endless. —**dear:** grievous.

---

† There seems to be a contradiction between narrative time and playing time immediately after Richard stops the duel. Although he and his council "withdraw" and then "return." his announcement of the decision follows quickly with seemingly no time allowed for what will sound like a fairly extended discussion. The earliest texts of the play provide nothing more than a flourish to cover the gap. In *Kings*, David William descends a flight of stairs, and with his back to the camera, seems to speak with three or four of his nobles; perhaps 15 or 20 seconds of film time elapse. Both *BBC* and *Bard* use a bit of camera trickery. After Richard and his council leave, both versions provide a few seconds of someone—Bolingbroke in *BBC*, the Marshall in *Bard*—waiting his return. Then, without changing the camera angle, the King is suddenly there. The effect of the jump cut is to create the sense that some indefinite period of time has been elided.

The hopeless word of "never to return"
Breathe I against thee, upon pain of life.

MOWBRY   A heavy sentence, my most sovereign liege,
And all unlook'd for from your Highness' mouth.   155
A dearer merit, not so deep a maim
As to be cast forth in the common air,
Have I deserved at your Highness' hands.
The language I have learnt these forty years,
My native English, now I must forgo;   160
And now my tongue's use is to me no more
Than an unstringed viol or a harp,
Or like a cunning instrument cas'd up
Or, being open, put into his hands
That knows no touch to tune the harmony.   165
Within my mouth you have enjail'd my tongue,
Doubly portcullis'd with my teeth and lips;
And dull, unfeeling, barren ignorance
Is made my jailer to attend on me.
I am too old to fawn upon a nurse,   170
Too far in years to be a pupil now.
What is thy sentence then but speechless death,
Which robs my tongue from breathing native breath?

KING   It boots thee not to be compassionate.
After our sentence plaining comes too late.   175

MOWBRY   Then thus I turn me from my country's light
To dwell in solemn shades of endless night.

KING   Return again and take an oath with thee.
Lay on our royal sword your banish'd hands;
Swear by the duty that you owe to God   180
(Our part therein we banish with yourselves)
To keep the oath that we administer:
You never shall, so help you truth and God,
Embrace each other's love in banishment;
Nor never look upon each other's face;   185
Nor never write, regreet, nor reconcile

152–53. **word:** sentence. **—Breathe:** pronounce. 155. **unlook'd for:** Mowbray had expected Richard to support him. 156. **a dearer merit:** a better recompense for my past services. 160. **forgo:** give up; renounce. 162. **viol:** a six-stringed instrument. 163. **cunning:** skilfully fashioned. 164. **being open:** out of its case [T.P.]. 167. **Doubly portcullis'd:** behind two grated gates [T.P.]. 171. **to be a pupil:** to learn to speak, as an infant learns from its nurse. 174–75. **boots:** profits, avails. **—to be compassionate:** to express pity for thyself in impassioned language **—plaining:** complaining; lamentation. 181. **Our part therin:** my share in your duty—your allegiance.

This low'ring tempest of your home-bred hate;
Nor never by advised purpose meet
To plot, contrive, or complot any ill
'Gainst us, our state, our subjects, or our land.   190

BOLINGBROKE   I swear.

MOWBRY   And I, to keep all this.

BOLINGBROKE   Norfolk, so far as to mine enemy:
By this time, had the King permitted us,
One of our souls had wand'red in the air,   195
Banish'd this frail sepulchre of our flesh,
As now our flesh is banish'd from this land.
Confess thy treasons ere thou fly the realm.
Since thou hast far to go, bear not along
The clogging burthen of a guilty soul.   200

MOWBRY   No, Bolingbroke. If ever I were traitor,
My name be blotted from the book of life
And I from heaven banish'd as from hence!
But what thou art, God, thou, and I do know;
And all too soon, I fear, the King shall rue.   205
Farewell, my liege. Now no way can I stray.
Save back to England, all the world's my way.   *Exit.*

KING   Uncle, even in the glasses of thine eyes
I see thy grieved heart. Thy sad aspect
Hath from the number of his banish'd years   210
Pluck'd four away. [*To Bolingbroke*] Six frozen winters spent,
Return with welcome home from banishment.

BOLINGBROKE   How long a time lies in one little word!
Four lagging winters and four wanton springs
End in a word, such is the breath of kings.   215

GAUNT   I thank my liege that in regard of me
He shortens four years of my son's exile.
But little vantage shall I reap thereby;
For ere the six years that he hath to spend
Can change their moons and bring their times about,   220

---

187. **regreet:** meet again. 188. **by advised purpose:** with deliberate intent. 189. **our state:** my royal government. 200. **clogging:** like a clog, a weight fastened to the leg of a prisoner [T.P.]. 205. **shall rue:** will learn—to his sorrow. 206–07. **Now no way can I stray...way:** Now I can never lose my way or wander from the right path, for—except for England—everywhere in the world is the road I am to travel. 214. **wanton:** sportive. 215. **such is the breath of kings:** such is the power that lies in the words of a king. 218. **vantage:** advantage, profit.

My oil-dried lamp and time-bewasted light
Shall be extinct with age and endless night,
My inch of taper will be burnt and done,
And blindfold death not let me see my son.

KING   Why, uncle, thou hast many years to live.   225

GAUNT   But not a minute, King, that thou canst give.
Shorten my days thou canst with sullen sorrow
And pluck nights from me, but not lend a morrow.
Thou canst help time to furrow me with age,
But stop no wrinkle in his pilgrimage.   230
Thy word is current with him for my death,
But dead, thy kingdom cannot buy my breath.

KING   Thy son is banish'd upon good advice,
Whereto thy tongue a party-verdict gave.
Why at our justice seem'st thou then to low'r?   235

GAUNT   Things sweet to taste prove in digestion sour.
You urg'd me as a judge; but I had rather
You would have bid me argue like a father.
O, had it been a stranger, not my child,
To smooth his fault I should have been more mild.   240
A partial slander sought I to avoid,
And in the sentence my own life destroy'd.
Alas, I look'd when some of you should say
I was too strict to make mine own away;
But you gave leave to my unwilling tongue   245
Against my will to do myself this wrong.

KING   Cousin, farewell; and, uncle, bid him so.
Six years we banish him, and he shall go.

Flourish. Exit [King with his Train].

AUMERLE   Cousin, farewell. What presence must not know,
From where you do remain let paper show.   250

MARSHAL   My lord, no leave take I; for I will ride,

---

222. **extinct:** extinguished. 223. **taper:** life's candle [T.P.]. 224. **blindfold death:** the blindness that death brings. 227–28. **sullen:** gloomy, brooding. —**a morrow:** a morning. 230. **stop...pilgrimage:** hinder not one wrinkle that the pilgrimage of my life brings to me. —**his:** i.e., time's. 231. **is current with him:** passes current with him; suffices to give him authority. 233–34. **upon good advice:** as the result of careful deliberation (by the King's Council). —**Whereto...gave:** and for his banishment you gave your verdict as one member of the Council. 237. **You urg'd me:** You called upon me for an opinion. 240. **smooth:** palliate, extenuate. 241. **A partial slander:** the reproach of partiality. 244. **I was too strict to make mine own away:** It was too strict an act on my part to make away with my own son [T.P.]. 246. **wrong:** injury, not injustice. 249–50. **What presence must not know:** what we are not allowed to learn from you in person. —**From...show:** inform us by letters from wherever you may be staying

As far as land will let me, by your side.

GAUNT O, to what purpose dost thou hoard thy words
That thou returnest no greeting to thy friends?†

BOLINGBROKE I have too few to take my leave of you, 255
When the tongue's office should be prodigal
To breathe the abundant dolour of the heart.

GAUNT Thy grief is but thy absence for a time.

BOLINGBROKE Joy absent, grief is present for that time.

GAUNT What is six winters? They are quickly gone. 260

BOLINGBROKE To men in joy; but grief makes one hour ten.

GAUNT Call it a travel that thou tak'st for pleasure.

BOLINGBROKE My heart will sigh when I miscall it so,
Which finds it an enforced pilgrimage.

GAUNT The sullen passage of thy weary steps 265
Esteem as foil wherein thou art to set
The precious jewel of thy home return.

BOLINGBROKE Nay, rather every tedious stride I make
Will but remember me what a deal of world
I wander from the jewels that I love. 270
Must I not serve a long apprenticehood
To foreign passages and, in the end,
Having my freedom, boast of nothing else
But that I was a journeyman to grief?

GAUNT All places that the eye of heaven visits 275
Are to a wise man ports and happy havens.
Teach thy necessity to reason thus:
There is no virtue like necessity.
Think not the King did banish thee,
But thou the King. Woe doth the heavier sit 280

---

257. **breathe:** utter, express. —**dolor:** grief. 265. **sullen:** slow and melancholy. 266. **foil:** a leaf of metal, used in the setting for a gem to enhance its brilliancy by contrast. 269. **remember:** remind. 271–74. **a long apprenticehood…a journeyman to grief:** The regular term during which an apprentice to any trade was bound by contract to serve his master was seven years. Then he "had his freedom" and became a journeyman. Bolingbroke must serve as apprentice to "foreign passages," i.e., must learn how to live in foreign lands, and, when he has thus won his "freedom," he will find that the trade he has learned is merely how to suffer.

---

† The final dialogue with Gaunt is as close as we ever come to a totally personal scene for Bolingbroke, who will never have a soliloquy or a conversation with a trusted confidant. All versions try to evoke something of the natural emotion of the parting of father and son. *BBC* creates a little more intimacy by shifting the scene to the interior of Bolingbroke's tent.

Where it perceives it is but faintly borne.
Go, say I sent thee forth to purchase honor,
And not, the King exil'd thee; or suppose
Devouring pestilence hangs in our air
And thou art flying to a fresher clime.   285
Look, what thy soul holds dear, imagine it
To lie that way thou goest, not whence thou com'st.
Suppose the singing birds musicians,
The grass whereon thou tread'st the presence strow'd,
The flowers fair ladies, and thy steps no more   290
Than a delightful measure or a dance;
For gnarling sorrow hath less power to bite
The man that mocks at it and sets it light.

BOLINGBROKE O, who can hold a fire in his hand
By thinking on the frosty Caucasus?   295
Or cloy the hungry edge of appetite
By bare imagination of a feast?
Or wallow naked in December snow
By thinking on fantastic summer's heat?
O, no! The apprehension of the good   300
Gives but the greater feeling to the worse.
Fell sorrow's tooth doth never rankle more
Than when he bites, but lanceth not the sore.

GAUNT Come, come, my son, I'll bring thee on thy way.
Had I thy youth and cause, I would not stay.   305

BOLINGBROKE Then, England's ground, farewell; sweet soil, adieu,
My mother, and my nurse, that bears me yet!
Where'er I wander, boast of this I can,
Though banish'd, yet a trueborn English man.   *Exeunt.*

---

281. **faintly:** feebly [T.P.]. 282. **purchase:** win. 286. **what:** whatever. 289. **the presence strow'd:** the King's presence chamber, carpeted with rushes. 291. **measure:** a stately dance or a figure (movement) in dancing. 292. **gnarling:** growling, snarling. 299. **fantastic:** imaginary. 300–01. **The apprehension of the good…worse:** the mind's conception (the idea) of what is good merely gives more poignancy to discomfort or misfortune. 302–03. **Fell:** fierce. —**rankle:** breed infection in a wound. —**lanceth:** as a surgeon lances a wound to relieve the patient. 304. **bring:** escort.

Scene IV. [*London. The court.*]

Enter the King, with Green and Bagot, at one door, and the Lord Aumerle at another.[†]

KING   We did observe. Cousin Aumerle,
              How far brought you high Hereford on his way?

AUMERLE   I brought high Hereford, if you call him so,
              But to the next high way, and there I left him.

KING   And say, what store of parting tears were shed?   5

AUMERLE   Faith, none for me; except the northeast wind,
              Which then blew bitterly against our faces,
              Awak'd the sleeping rheum, and so by chance
              Did grace our hollow parting with a tear.

KING   What said our cousin when you parted with him?   10

AUMERLE   "Farewell!"
              And, for my heart disdained that my tongue
              Should so profane the word, that taught me craft
              To counterfeit oppression of such grief
              That words seem'd buried in my sorrow's grave.   15
              Marry, would the word "farewell" have length'ned hours
              And added years to his short banishment,
              He should have had a volume of farewells;
              But since it would not, he had none of me.

KING   He is our cousin, cousin; but 'tis doubt,   20
              When time shall call him home from banishment,
              Whether our kinsman come to see his friends.
              Ourself and Bushy, Bagot here, and Green
              Observ'd his courtship to the common people;

ACT I. SCENE IV.
1. **We did observe:** Referring to something about Bolingbroke that Green or Bagot has said to the King as they enter. —**cousin:** The Duke of Aumerle was Richard's own cousin. 6. **for me:** on my part. —**except:** unless perhaps. 8. **the sleeping rheum:** the dormant moisture. 12. **for:** because. 14. **counterfeit:** pretend [T.P.]. 16. **Marry:** Literally, an oath by the Virgin Mary, but regularly used as a light interjection. 18–19. **should:** would certainly. —**of me:** from me.

---

†   Like 1.2, an intimate scene following a public scene and one that begins in mid conversation. Richard among his friends can comfortably admit his extravagance, his suspicion of Bolingbroke, his continual gouging of his subjects, and even his plan to expropriate Gaunt's estate. Both *BBC* and *Bard* emphasize the intimacy. In *BBC*, the setting is a bath house in which Richard, in something like a nightshirt, is receiving a massage from Green, who is naked but for a towel around his waist; Bagot soaks in a tub. *Bard* begins with Richard nude on a chaise lounge with only a gold cloth over his privates. As in *BBC*, he puts on a light gown, receives a shoulder massage, and even rubs lotion on his hands and face, Both versions seem to flirt with the implication of homosexuality. *Kings*, on the other hand, has Richard at the same desk he used in 1.1, signing papers.

In an unlikely setting, Green (Alan Dalton) is actually discussing the rebellion in Ireland with King Richard (Derek Jacobi). (*BBC*, 1978.)

How he did seem to dive into their hearts   25
With humble and familiar courtesy;
What reverence he did throw away on slaves,
Wooing poor craftsmen with the craft of smiles
And patient underbearing of his fortune,
As 'twere to banish their affects with him.   30
Off goes his bonnet to an oyster-wench;
A brace of draymen bid God speed him well
And had the tribute of his supple knee,
With "Thanks, my countrymen, my loving friends";
As were our England in reversion his,   35
And he our subjects' next degree in hope.

---

29. **patient underbearing:** calm endurance. 30. **as 'twere...with him:** as if he were trying to carry the affections of the common people away with him in his banishment. 31. **bonnet:** hat, cap. 32. **bid God speed him well:** prayed God to give him prosperous fortune. 33. **had the tribute of his supple knee:** were rewarded with the bending of his knee in an elaborate bow. 35. **in reversion his:** his by right of legal possession as soon as my tenancy expires.

GREEN	Well, he is gone, and with him go these thoughts!
	Now for the rebels which stand out in Ireland,
	Expedient manage must be made, my liege,
	Ere further leisure yield them further means	40
	For their advantage and your Highness' loss.

KING   We will ourself in person to this war;
And, for our coffers, with too great a court
And liberal largess, are grown somewhat light,
We are enforc'd to farm our royal realm,   45
The revenue whereof shall furnish us
For our affairs in hand. If that come short,
Our substitutes at home shall have blank charters,
Whereto, when they shall know what men are rich,
They shall subscribe them for large sums of gold   50
And send them after to supply our wants,
For we will make for Ireland presently.

                    Enter Bushy.[†]

Bushy, what news?

BUSHY   Old John of Gaunt is grievous sick, my lord,
Suddenly taken, and hath sent post-haste   55
To entreat your Majesty to visit him.

KING   Where lies he?

BUSHY   At Ely House.

KING   Now put it, God, in the physician's mind
To help him to his grave immediately!   60
The lining of his coffers shall make coats
To deck our soldiers for these Irish wars.
Come, gentlemen, let's all go visit him.
Pray God we may make haste, and come too late!

ALL   Amen.   *Exeunt.* 65

38–39. **stand out:** are in insurrection. —**Expedient manage must be made:** Speedy measures must be taken. 42. **to:** go to. 43. **with too great a court:** because of my keeping too many retainers. 44. **liberal largess:** lavish gifts. 45. **to farm our royal realm:** to lease for rent—the lessees having the right to collect all the revenues for their own use. 48. **Our substitutes at home:** the deputies to whom the government of the realm is assigned during my absence. —**charters:** writs for the collection of revenue. 50. **subscribe them:** enter their names (in the blank spaces in the charters). 52. **presently:** immediately. 55. **taken:** taken ill [T.P.]. 61. **the lining of his coffers:** the money with which his coffers (strongboxes [T.P.]) are furnished. —**coats:** coats of mail.

---

†   In John Farrell's 2001 version, Bushy reads Sonnet 29 to the King and Queen's applause.

York (Charles Gray) and the dying Gaunt (John Gielgud) lament Richard's misrule. (*BBC*, 1978.)

ACT II

Scene I. [*London. Ely House.*]

Enter John of Gaunt, sick, with the Duke of York &c.

GAUNT	Will the King come, that I may breathe my last	
	In wholesome counsel to his unstaid youth?[†]	
YORK	Vex not yourself nor strive not with your breath,	
	For all in vain comes counsel to his ear.	
GAUNT	O, but they say the tongues of dying men	5
	Enforce attention like deep harmony.	

ACT II. SCENE I.
2. **unstaid:** unrestrained (T.P.).

---

† All three versions begin with the dying Gaunt in a chair. In Shakespeare's theater, he would most likely have been carried on and off stage in the chair. Since usually only the King is seated, this scene can suggest a reversal of the usual authority. It is presumably to avoid this implication that in *BBC* Gielgud as Gaunt stands once Richard enters, and remains standing while he criticizes Richard's behavior.

Where words are scarce, they are seldom spent in vain,
For they breathe truth that breathe their words in pain.
He that no more must say is listened more
Than they whom youth and ease have taught to glose.   10
More are men's ends mark'd than their lives before.
The setting sun, and music at the close,
As the last taste of sweets, is sweetest last,
Writ in remembrance more than things long past.
Though Richard my live's counsel would not hear,   15
My death's sad tale may yet undeaf his ear.

YORK   No; it is stopp'd with other flattering sounds,
As praises, of whose taste the wise are fond,
Lascivious metres, to whose venom sound
The open ear of youth doth always listen;   20
Report of fashions in proud Italy,
Whose manners still our tardy apish nation
Limps after in base imitation.
Where doth the world thrust forth a vanity
(So it be new, there's no respect how vile)   25
That is not quickly buzz'd into his ears?
Then all too late comes counsel to be heard
Where will doth mutiny with wit's regard.
Direct not him whose way himself will choose.
'Tis breath thou lack'st, and that breath wilt thou lose.   30

GAUNT   Methinks I am a prophet new inspir'd
And thus, expiring, do foretell of him:
His rash fierce blaze of riot cannot last,
For violent fires soon burn out themselves;
Small show'rs last long, but sudden storms are short;   35
He tires betimes that spurs too fast betimes;
With eager feeding food doth choke the feeder;
Light vanity, insatiate cormorant,

---

8. **breathe:** utter. 9. **listened:** heeded [T.P.]. 10. **to glose:** literally, "to flatter;" here "to use pleasant language and talk about agreeable things." 13. **is sweetest last:** is longest remembered as sweet. 14. **writ in remembrance:** set down (as if in writing) in the memory. 15. **my live's counsel:** my advice while I lived. 16. **My death's sad tale:** the serious words that I speak on my deathbed. 17. **other flattering sounds:** with other pleasing sounds. 19. **meters:** songs. —**venom:** poisonous. 21. **proud:** gorgeous. Used especially to denote lavish splendor in attire. 22. **still:** ever, always. —**tardy apish:** imitative—though lagging far behind our model. 24–25. **thrust forth a vanity:** exhibit any piece of showy extravagance. —**So:** provided that; if only. —**vile:** contemptible, worthless. 26. **buzz'd into his ears:** reported to him by his flattering courtiers. 28. **Where will...regard:** where one's desires rise in rebellion against all considerations of wisdom or common sense. 29. **whose way himself will choose:** who insists on choosing his own course. 33–34. **riot:** riotous living; dissipation. 36. **He tires betimes...betimes:** He soon tires who rides too fast early in the day, at the beginning of the day's travel.

Consuming means, soon preys upon itself.
This royal throne of kings, this scept'red isle,   40
This earth of majesty, this seat of Mars,
This other Eden, demi-paradise,
This fortress built by Nature for herself
Against infection and the hand of war,
This happy breed of men, this little world,   45
This precious stone set in the silver sea,
Which serves it in the office of a wall,
Or as a moat defensive to a house,
Against the envy of less happier lands;
This blessed plot, this earth, this realm, this England,   50
This nurse, this teeming womb of royal kings,
Fear'd by their breed and famous by their birth,
Renowned for their deeds as far from home,
For Christian service and true chivalry,
As is the sepulchre in stubborn Jewry   55
Of the world's ransom, blessed Mary's son;
This land of such dear souls, this dear dear land,
Dear for her reputation through the world,
Is now leas'd out (I die pronouncing it)
Like to a tenement or pelting farm.   60
England, bound in with the triumphant sea,
Whose rocky shore beats back the envious siege
Of wat'ry Neptune, is now bound in with shame,
With inky blots and rotten parchment bonds.
That England that was wont to conquer others   65
Hath made a shameful conquest of itself.
Ah, would the scandal vanish with my life,
How happy then were my ensuing death!

Enter King, Queen, Aumerle, Bushy, Green, Bagot, Ross, and Willoughby.

YORK   The King is come. Deal mildly with his youth;
            For young hot colts, being rag'd, do rage the more.   70

QUEEN   How fares our noble uncle Lancaster?

---

41. **other:** second. —**demiparadise:** paradise in miniature. 38. **cormorant:** a traditionally greedy bird. 47. **serves it in the office:** does it the special service. 49. **envy:** enmity, hostility. 52. **Fear'd by their breed:** held in awe by reason of their warlike ancestry. 55. **Jewry:** Judea. 56. **the world's ransom:** the Savior who redeemed the world by his death. 60. **a tenement:** a piece of real estate held by a tenant. —**pelting:** paltry, insignificant. 62. **envious:** hostile. 63–64. **bound in with shame:** confined (restricted in her natural rights) by shameful fetters. —**inky blots:** a contemptuous term for writings. 68. **my ensuing death!:** my death, however quickly it might follow! 70. **being rag'd:** roughly handled.

KING	What comfort, man? How is't with aged Gaunt?
GAUNT	O, how that name befits my composition!
	Old Gaunt indeed, and gaunt in being old.
	Within me grief hath kept a tedious fast; 75
	And who abstains from meat that is not gaunt?
	For sleeping England long time have I watch'd;
	Watching breeds leanness, leanness is all gaunt.
	The pleasure that some fathers feed upon
	Is my strict fast—I mean my children's looks— 80
	And therein fasting hast thou made me gaunt.
	Gaunt am I for the grave, gaunt as a grave,
	Whose hollow womb inherits naught but bones.
KING	Can sick men play so nicely with their names?
GAUNT	No, misery makes sport to mock itself. 85
	Since thou dost seek to kill my name in me,
	I mock my name, great King, to flatter thee.
KING	Should dying men flatter with those that live?
GAUNT	No, no! men living flatter those that die.
KING	Thou, now a-dying, say'st thou flatterest me. 90
GAUNT	O, no! thou diest, though I the sicker be.
KING	I am in health, I breathe, and see thee ill.
GAUNT	Now, he that made me knows I see thee ill;
	Ill in myself to see, and in thee seeing ill.
	Thy deathbed is no lesser than thy land, 95
	Wherein thou liest in reputation sick;
	And thou, too careless patient as thou art,
	Committ'st thy anointed body to the cure
	Of those physicians that first wounded thee.

---

72. **What comfort?:** A form of enquiry about one's health. 73. **my composition:** the state of my health. 75–76. **Within...fast:** The grief that is within me has made me fast a long time. —**meat:** food. 77. **watch'd:** kept awake; gone without sleep. 80. **Is my strict fast:** is something from which I have been forced to abstain. 81. **therein fasting:** "You have made me gaunt because I have had to fast in that respect." 82. **Gaunt am I for the grave:** wasted away to the point of death. 83. **inherits:** possesses. 84. **so nicely:** with such witty trifling. 85.**to mock itself:** by making itself the object of jests. 86. **to kill my name in me:** to make my name die with me by depriving me of my heir, since my son is banished. 94. **Ill in myself to see and in thee seeing ill:** made sick at heart by the sight of your illness—i.e., abuse of kingly power and subjection to disloyal favorites. 99. **those physicians that first wounded thee:** your corrupt favorites.

A thousand flatterers sit within thy crown,   100
Whose compass is no bigger than thy head;
And yet, incaged in so small a verge,
The waste is no whit lesser than thy land.
O, had thy grandsire, with a prophet's eye,
Seen how his son's son should destroy his sons,   105
From forth thy reach he would have laid thy shame,
Deposing thee before thou wert possess'd,
Which art possess'd now to depose thyself.
Why, cousin, wert thou regent of the world,
It were a shame to let this land by lease;   110
But, for thy world enjoying but this land,
Is it not more than shame to shame it so?
Landlord of England art thou now, not King.
Thy state of law is bondslave to the law,
And thou—

KING   A lunatic lean-witted fool,   115
Presuming on an ague's privilege,
Dar'st with thy frozen admonition
Make pale our cheek, chasing the royal blood
With fury from his native residence.
Now, by my seat's right royal majesty,   120
Wert thou not brother to great Edward's son,
This tongue that runs so roundly in thy head
Should run thy head from thy unreverent shoulders.

GAUNT   O, spare me not, my brother Edward's son,
For that I was his father Edward's son!   125
That blood already, like the pelican,
Hast thou tapp'd out and drunkenly carous'd.
My brother Gloucester, plain well-meaning soul
(Whom fair befall in heaven 'mongst happy souls!),

100–03. **A thousand flatterers…thy land:** The royal power is administered by countless flatterers, who may be called the occupants of thy crown, since they usurp the crown's authority. —**verge:** boundary, limit. 104. **thy grandsire:** Edward III, whom Richard had succeeded [T.P.]. 105. **should:** was to. 106. **From forth:** out of. 107. **wert possess'd:** came into possession of the throne 108. **possess'd:** governed by an insane impulse—literally, possessed by a devil. —**to depose thyself:** by allowing thyself to be ruled by thy favorites and letting out the whole realm on lease. 114. **Thy state…to the law:** Your legal status is no longer that of supreme King of England by divine right; for you are now as subject to the law in regard to the whole realm as any landlord is with reference to his private estate. 116. **an ague's privilege:** a dying man's right to use plain language. 122. **so roundly:** in such blunt language. 125. **For that:** because. —**his father Edward's son:** the son of Edward III, who was the father of your father—my brother Edward the Black Prince. 126–27. **like the pelican:** The mother pelican supposedly pecks open her breast to feed her young with her heart's blood, and is therefore an emblem of parental care. Gaunt imagines the pecking open is done by the young pelican, thus signifying viciously unfilial behavior [T.P]. 127. **carous'd:** drunk down in great draughts.

	May be a precedent and witness good	130
	That thou respect'st not spilling Edward's blood.	
	Join with the present sickness that I have,	
	And thy unkindness be like crooked age,	
	To crop at once a too long withered flower.	
	Live in thy shame, but die not shame with thee!	135
	These words hereafter thy tormenters be!	
	Convey me to my bed, then to my grave.	
	Love they to live that love and honor have.	

Exit [borne off by Attendants].

KING   And let them die that age and sullens have;
            For both hast thou, and both become the grave.   140

YORK   I do beseech your Majesty, impute his words
            To wayward sickliness and age in him.
            He loves you, on my life, and holds you dear
            As Harry Duke of Hereford, were he here.

KING   Right, you say true! As Hereford's love, so his;   145
            As theirs, so mine; and all be as it is!

Enter Northumberland.

NORTHUMBERLAND My liege, old Gaunt commends him to your Majesty.

KING   What says he?

NORTHUMBERLAND   Nay, nothing; all is said.
            His tongue is now a stringless instrument;
            Words, life, and all, old Lancaster hath spent.   150

YORK   Be York the next that must be bankrout so!
            Though death be poor, it ends a mortal woe.

KING   The ripest fruit first falls, and so doth he;
            His time is spent, our pilgrimage must be.
            So much for that. Now for our Irish wars.   155
            We must supplant those rough rug-headed kerns,
            Which live like venom where no venom else
            But only they have privilege to live.
            And, for these great affairs do ask some charge,

---

130. **may be a precedent:** may serve as an example. 131. **respect'st not:** feel no scruples about. 133. **thy unkindness be:** let your unkindness serve. 138. **Love they to live:** Let those love to live. 139. **sullens:** sullenness [T.P.]. 143–45. **dear As Harry:** as dear as he holds Harry. —**As Hereford's love:** as Hereford's love to me. The King ironically twists the sense of York's words. 147. **commends him:** sends his respectful greetings. 151–52. **be bankrout so!:** be bankrupt in that way—i.e., by having spent words, life, and all. 154. **our pilgrimage:** my life, my future [T.P.]. 156. **supplant:** expel, drive out. —**rug-headed:** shaggy-haired —**kerns:** light-armed Irish soldiers. 157. **no venom else:** no other venomous reptiles. 159. **for:** because.

	Towards our assistance we do seize to us	160
	The plate, coin, revenues, and moveables	
	Whereof our uncle Gaunt did stand possess'd.	

YORK   How long shall I be patient? Ah, how long
Shall tender duty make me suffer wrong?
Not Gloucester's death, nor Hereford's banishment,   165
Nor Gaunt's rebukes, nor England's private wrongs,
Nor the prevention of poor Bolingbroke
About his marriage, nor my own disgrace,
Have ever made me sour my patient cheek
Or bend one wrinkle on my sovereign's face.   170
I am the last of noble Edward's sons,
Of whom thy father, Prince of Wales, was first.
In war was never lion rag'd more fierce,
In peace was never gentle lamb more mild,
Than was that young and princely gentleman.   175
His face thou hast, for even so look'd he,
Accomplish'd with the number of thy hours;
But when he frown'd, it was against the French
And not against his friends. His noble hand
Did win what he did spend, and spent not that   180
Which his triumphant father's hand had won.
His hands were guilty of no kinred blood,
But bloody with the enemies of his kin.
O Richard! York is too far gone with grief,
Or else he never would compare between.   185

KING   Why, uncle, what's the matter?

YORK   O my liege,
Pardon me, if you please; if not, I, pleas'd
Not to be pardoned, am content withal.
Seek you to seize and gripe into your hands
The royalties and rights of banish'd Hereford?   190
Is not Gaunt dead? and doth not Hereford live?
Was not Gaunt just? and is not Harry true?
Did not the one deserve to have an heir?

---

161. **plate:** gold and silver utensils [T.P.]. —**moveables:** portable property [T.P.]. 164. **tender duty:** scrupulous regard for my duty to my King. 166. **Gaunt's rebukes:** the King's rebukes of Gaunt. —**England's private wrongs:** the wrongs which private citizens have had to suffer throughout England. 167–68. **The prevention...marriage:** Richard had prohibited Bolingbroke from marrying a niece of the French King Charles VI, not otherwise mentioned in the play [T.P.]. 170. **bend one wrinkle on:** direct one suggestion of a frown at. 172. **Prince of Wales:** Edward the Black Prince (see 2.3.101, note). 177. **Accomplish'd... hours:** when he had arrived at your present age. King Richard was thirty-two years old. 182. **kinred:** kindred. 188. **withal:** with it—i.e., with not being pardoned. 190. **royalties:** privileges granted by a king. 192. **just:** righteous in all his dealings. —**true:** loyal.

Is not his heir a well-deserving son?
Take Hereford's rights away, and take from Time   195
His charters and his customary rights;
Let not tomorrow then ensue today;
Be not thyself—for how art thou a king
But by fair sequence and succession?
Now, afore God (God forbid I say true!),   200
If you do wrongfully seize Hereford's rights,
Call in the letters patents that he hath
By his attorneys general to sue
His livery, and deny his off'red homage,
You pluck a thousand dangers on your head,   205
You lose a thousand well-disposed hearts,
And prick my tender patience to those thoughts
Which honor and allegiance cannot think.

KING   Think what you will, we seize into our hands
              His plate, his goods, his money, and his lands.   210

YORK   I'll not be by the while. My liege, farewell.
              What will ensue hereof there's none can tell;
              But by bad courses may be understood
              That their events can never fall out good.   *Exit.*

KING   Go, Bushy, to the Earl of Wiltshire straight.   215
              Bid him repair to us to Ely House
              To see this business. Tomorrow next
              We will for Ireland; and 'tis time, I trow.
              And we create, in absence of ourself,
              Our uncle York Lord Governor of England;   220
              For he is just and always lov'd us well.
              Come on, our queen. Tomorrow must we part.
              Be merry, for our time of stay is short.

                                              Flourish. Exeunt.

---

195. **from Time:** since Hereford's rights have come to him by succession—in the inevitable course of time. 200. **God forbid I say true!:** I pray God that what I am saying may not come true! 202–04. **Call in the letters patents:** revoke the royal grant. —**By his attorneys...livery:** the royal grant that gives him the right to make suit by means of his attorneys for the delivery to him of the lands that his father held as tenant of the crown. Such a suit was the regular proceeding to establish the heir's full age and his right to inheritance. —**deny:** refuse to accept. —**homage:** For Bolingbroke to do homage to the King would be part of the ceremony attending the delivery of the lands. 207. **prick:** spur on; incite. —**patience:** self-control. 211. **by:** near by; present. 212–14. **ensue hereof:** be the result of this. —**by:** concerning, with regard to. —**events:** results; the outcome. 215. **the Earl of Wiltshire:** Wiltshire was historically Richard's Lord Treasurer and prominent among his creditors. He is often mentioned in the play as one of Richard's "flatterers," and his execution is reported in 3.4, but he never appears on stage [T.P.]. —**straight:** straightway, immediately. 217. **see:** see to; attend to. 218. **will for:** will start for. —**'tis time, I trow:** it's high time, I think. 219. **ourself:** myself, the King.

Manent Northumberland, Willoughby, and Ross.

NORTHUMBERLAND Well, lords, the Duke of Lancaster is dead.

ROSS   And living too; for now his son is Duke.   225

WILLOUGHBY   Barely in title, not in revenues.

NORTHUMBERLAND Richly in both, if justice had her right.

ROSS   My heart is great; but it must break with silence,
              Ere 't be disburdened with a liberal tongue.

NORTHUMBERLAND Nay, speak thy mind; and let him ne'er speak more   230
              That speaks thy words again to do thee harm!

WILLOUGHBY   Tends that thou wouldst speak to the Duke of Hereford?
              If it be so, out with it boldly, man!
              Quick is mine ear to hear of good towards him.

ROSS   No good at all that I can do for him;   235
              Unless you call it good to pity him,
              Bereft and gelded of his patrimony.

NORTHUMBERLAND Now, afore God, 'tis shame such wrongs are borne
              In him a royal prince and many moe
              Of noble blood in this declining land.   240
              The King is not himself, but basely led
              By flatterers; and what they will inform,
              Merely in hate, 'gainst any of us all,
              That will the King severely prosecute
              'Gainst us, our lives, our children, and our heirs.   245

ROSS   The commons hath he pill'd with grievous taxes
              And quite lost their hearts; the nobles hath he fin'd
              For ancient quarrels and quite lost their hearts.

WILLOUGHBY   And daily new exactions are devis'd,
              As blanks, benevolences, and I wot not what;   250
              But what, a God's name, doth become of this?

NORTHUMBERLAND Wars have not wasted it, for warr'd he hath not,
              But basely yielded upon compromise

---

226. **Barely:** He is *barely* Duke of Lancaster; for he has only the *bare title*, and even that is *barely* (scarcely) in his possession, since he is a banished man. 228. **great:** swollen with grief and indignation. 229. **with a liberal tongue:** *Liberal* suggests not merely free speech but language that would be too outspoken to be prudent. 232. **Tends...to:** has reference to. 238–39. **wrongs...In him:** i.e., wrongs in his case—royal prince though he is. —**moe:** more [T.P.]. 242. **what they will inform:** whatsoever false information they choose to bring. 246. **pill'd:** stripped bare—literally, peeled. 250. **benevolences:** The mild and specious term for "forced loans"—as if these were kindly gifts to assist the King. —**wot:** know. 251. **a God's name:** in God's name. —**doth become of this?:** becomes of all this money?

| | That which his noble ancestors achiev'd with blows. | |
| | More hath he spent in peace than they in wars. | 255 |

Ross   The Earl of Wiltshire hath the realm in farm.

Willoughby   The King's grown bankrout, like a broken man.

Northumberland   Reproach and dissolution hangeth over him.

Ross   He hath not money for these Irish wars,
His burthenous taxations notwithstanding,   260
But by the robbing of the banish'd Duke.

Northumberland   His noble kinsman. Most degenerate king!
But, lords, we hear this fearful tempest sing,
Yet seek no shelter to avoid the storm.
We see the wind sit sore upon our sails,   265
And yet we strike not, but securely perish.

Ross   We see the very wrack that we must suffer,
And unavoided is the danger now
For suffering so the causes of our wrack.

Northumberland   Not so. Even through the hollow eyes of death   270
I spy life peering; but I dare not say
How near the tidings of our comfort is.

Willoughby   Nay, let us share thy thoughts as thou dost ours.

Ross   Be confident to speak, Northumberland.
We three are but thyself, and speaking so,   275
Thy words are but as thoughts. Therefore be bold.

Northumberland   Then thus: I have from Le Port Blanc, a bay
In Britain, receiv'd intelligence
That Harry Duke of Hereford, Rainold Lord Cobham,

.   .   .   .   280

That late broke from the Duke of Exeter,
His brother, Archbishop late of Canterbury,
Sir Thomas Erpingham, Sir John Ramston,
Sir John Norbery, Sir Robert Waterton, and Francis Quoint,
All these well furnish'd by the Duke of Britain   285
With eight tall ships, three thousand men of war,

---

254. **achiev'd:** won. 256. **in farm:** on lease. 257. **bankrout:** bankrupt. 258. **Reproach and dissolution:** a shameful and fatal end of life. 260. **burthenous:** burdensome. 265. **sit sore:** weigh heavily. 266. **strike not:** do not strike sail. —**securely:** heedlessly; without thought of danger. 268–269. **unavoided:** unavoidable. —**For suffering so...wrack:** because we have thus allowed the causes of our ruin to go on unchecked. *Suffering* means "permitting." 278. **Britain:** Brittany. 279. **Rainold:** Reginald. 280. A line has dropped out here. Many editors insert Edmond Malone's plausible guess "The son of Richard Earl of Arundel," who did in fact break from the Duke of Exeter. [T.P.]. 286. **tall:** gallant, stately. —**men of war:** soldiers.

Are making hither with all due expedience
And shortly mean to touch our northern shore.†
Perhaps they had ere this, but that they stay
The first departing of the King for Ireland.   290
If then we shall shake off our slavish yoke,
Imp out our drooping country's broken wing,
Redeem from broking pawn the blemish'd crown,
Wipe off the dust that hides our sceptre's gilt,
And make high majesty look like itself,   295
Away with me in post to Ravenspurgh;
But if you faint, as fearing to do so,
Stay and be secret, and myself will go.

Ross   To horse, to horse! Urge doubts to them that fear.

WILLOUGHBY   Hold out my horse, and I will first be there.‡   *Exeunt.* 300

Scene II. [*Windsor Castle.*]

BUSHY   Madam, your Majesty is too much sad.§
                You promis'd, when you parted with the King,
                To lay aside life-harming heaviness
                And entertain a cheerful disposition.

QUEEN   To please the King, I did; to please myself,   5
                I cannot do it. Yet I know no cause

287. **due expedience:** proper speed. 289. **had:** would have (landed). 291–93. **shall:** are to. **—Imp out:** A technical term in falconry: "mend by grafting new feathers." **—from broking pawn:** from being pledged to pawnbrokers. 294. **gilt:** golden luster. 296. **in post:** posthaste; at full speed 297. **faint:** lack energy. 299. **Urge:** mention; speak of. 300. **Hold out my horse:** i.e., if my horse does not fail me.

ACT II. SCENE II.
3–4. **heaviness:** melancholy. **—entertain a cheerful disposition:** take to yourself, instead, a cheerful frame of mind.

†   The final sequence among Northumberland, Willoughby, and Ross—for whom *Bard* substitutes Exton—appears to create a temporal contradiction. According to Northumberland, Bolingbroke is already on his way back from exile to reclaim his inheritance, apparently only moments after it has been seized. Some critics claim that we are meant to think that Bolingbroke has sailed from France even before his father's death, although the play's action from the time of his exile in 1.3 is so tightly consecutive that if all the indications are taken at face value, Bolingbroke would have had to sail from France before he has had time to leave England. *BBC* lessens the seeming contradiction by putting the three lords in a new location, on a balcony, while a precession that could be Gaunt's funeral passes below, thus suggesting the possibility of some time having passed.

‡   Both *Kings* and *Bard* play the scene immediately after Richard's exit and in the same place. *Kings* later on, however, will indicate a lapse of time by having Bolingbroke, who was clean shaven when he was exiled, return in 2.3 with a mustache and beard.

§   Only *Bard* plays the opening, rather over-complicated dialogue in which Bushy tries to dispel the Queen's premonition of disaster. Oddly, the actress (Mary Jane Negro) leans back on her pillows, smiling serenely at both the beginning and the end of the conversation.

Why I should welcome such a guest as grief
Save bidding farewell to so sweet a guest
As my sweet Richard. Yet again, methinks,
Some unborn sorrow, ripe in fortune's womb,   10
Is coming towards me, and my inward soul
With nothing trembles. At something it grieves
More than with parting from my lord the King.

BUSHY   Each substance of a grief hath twenty shadows,
Which shows like grief itself, but is not so;   15
For sorrow's eye, glazed with blinding tears,
Divides one thing entire to many objects,
Like perspectives, which rightly gaz'd upon,
Show nothing but confusion—ey'd awry,
Distinguish form. So your sweet Majesty,   20
Looking awry upon your lord's departure,
Find shapes of grief more than himself to wail,
Which, look'd on as it is, is naught but shadows
Of what it is not. Then, thrice-gracious Queen,
More than your lord's departure weep not. More's not seen;   25
Or if it be, 'tis with false sorrow's eye,
Which for things true weeps things imaginary.

QUEEN   It may be so; but yet my inward soul
Persuades me it is otherwise. Howe'er it be,
I cannot but be sad—so heavy sad   30
As, though in thinking on no thought I think,
Makes me with heavy nothing faint and shrink.

BUSHY   'Tis nothing but conceit, my gracious lady.

QUEEN   'Tis nothing less. Conceit is still deriv'd
From some forefather grief. Mine is not so,   35
For nothing hath begot my something grief,
Or something hath the nothing that I grieve.

11–12. **my inward soul With nothing trembles:** The very soul within me shudders, though I know no reason for fear. 14–15. **Each substance...so:** Every actual cause of sorrow casts twenty shadows of itself, each of which looks like a real cause of grief, but is only imaginary. 17–27. **Divides one thing, etc.:** Bushy compares the tear-glazed eye to a perspective glass. These were optical toys which distorted objects in various ways. So you, looking askance (i.e., with an eye of disfavor or unwillingness) upon the King's departure, see many other shapes of sorrow to wail at. If, however, you look with accurate sight, you find that it consists of nothing but shadows of unreality. Then weep for your lord's departure only. 28. **my inward soul:** my inmost soul. 31–32. **As...shrink:** so heavily depressed that—though in my mind I frame no definite thought of anything to cause sadness—I am made faint and tremulous by my causeless sorrow. 33. **conceit:** imagination. 34–37. **Conceit...forefather grief:** Grief that is due to imagination is always derived from some actual grief that has been felt in the past. **—Mine is not so, etc.:** My cause of grief is not actual.

'Tis in reversion that I do possess;
But what it is that is not yet known what,
I cannot name. 'Tis nameless woe, I wot.   40

Enter Green.

GREEN   God save your Majesty! and well met, gentlemen.†
           I hope the King is not yet shipp'd for Ireland.

QUEEN   Why hopest thou so? 'Tis better hope he is;
           For his designs crave haste, his haste good hope.
           Then wherefore dost thou hope he is not shipp'd?   45

GREEN   That he, our hope, might have retir'd his power
           And driven into despair an enemy's hope
           Who strongly hath set footing in this land.
           The banish'd Bolingbroke repeals himself
           And with uplifted arms is safe arriv'd   50
           At Ravenspurgh.

QUEEN   Now God in heaven forbid!

GREEN   Ah, madam, 'tis too true; and that is worse,
           The Lord Northumberland, his son young Henry Percy,
           The Lords of Ross, Beaumond, and Willoughby,
           With all their powerful friends, are fled to him.   55

BUSHY   Why have you not proclaim'd Northumberland
           And all the rest revolted faction traitors?

GREEN   We have; whereupon the Earl of Worcester
           Hath broken his staff, resign'd his stewardship,
           And all the household servants fled with him to Bolingbroke.   60

QUEEN   So, Green, thou art the midwife to my woe,
           And Bolingbroke my sorrow's dismal heir.
           Now hath my soul brought forth her prodigy;
           And I, a gasping new-deliver'd mother,

38–40. **'Tis in reversion...wot:** My grief is like a reversionary interest in an estate—something I will in time possess; as yet I do not know and cannot name what it is [T.P.]. 44. **crave:** need; call for. —**his haste good hope:** the fact that haste is necessary calls for hope that he has shipped. 46. **retir'd his power:** led back his army. 48. **strongly:** with a strong force 49. **repeals himself:** calls *himself* back from banishment. 50. **uplifted:** brandished. 52. **that:** what. 61–65. **the midwife:** since you have revealed the unknown cause of my sorrow. Bolingbroke, then, is the child that has been born. —**dismal:** ill-omened. —**heir:** eldest offspring.

---

†   *Kings* begins the scene at Green's arrival with the bad news that Bolingbroke has returned, and *BBC* cuts about the first hundred lines to give us York well into his lamenting the situation. All three versions clearly present Richard's favorites as committed only to saving their own skins. In *Kings*, Green seems to want to take the silverware with him.

| | Have woe to woe, sorrow to sorrow join'd. | 65 |

BUSHY   Despair not, madam.

QUEEN   Who shall hinder me?
I will despair, and be at enmity
With cozening Hope. He is a flatterer,
A parasite, a keeper-back of Death,
Who gently would dissolve the bands of life,   70
Which false hope lingers in extremity.

Enter York.

GREEN   Here comes the Duke of York.

QUEEN   With signs of war about his aged neck.
O, full of careful business are his looks.
Uncle, for God's sake, speak comfortable words!   75

YORK   Should I do so, I should belie my thoughts.
Comfort's in heaven, and we are on the earth,
Where nothing lives but crosses, cares, and grief.
Your husband, he is gone to save far off,
Whilst others come to make him lose at home.   80
Here am I left to underprop his land,
Who, weak with age, cannot support myself.
Now comes the sick hour that his surfeit made,
Now shall he try his friends that flatter'd him.

Enter a Servingman.

SERVANT   My lord, your son was gone before I came.   85

YORK   He was? Why, so! Go all which way it will!
The nobles they are fled, the commons they are cold
And will, I fear, revolt on Hereford's side.
Sirrah, get thee to Plashy to my sister Gloucester;
Bid her send me presently a thousand pound.   90
Hold, take my ring.

SERVANT   My lord, I had forgot to tell your lordship
Today, as I came by, I called there—
But I shall grieve you to report the rest.

YORK   What is't, knave?   95

---

68. **cozening:** deceitful. 71. **lingers in extremity:** causes to linger at the point of death. 73. **signs of war:** attire that indicates war. York wears a gorget—a piece of mail that defends the throat. 74. **careful:** distressful, anxious. 75. **comfortable:** comforting, encouraging. 78. **crosses:** thwarting circumstances. 83. **his surfeit:** his riotous conduct as king—literally, overfeeding. 84. **try:** test. 86. **so!:** so be it! 89. **Sirrah:** Often used in addressing a servant. —**my sister Gloucester:** i.e, my sister-in-law, the Duchess of Gloucester [T.P.]. 90. **presently:** immediately.

SERVANT   An hour before I came the Duchess died.

YORK   God for his mercy! What a tide of woes
Comes rushing on this woeful land at once!
I know not what to do. I would to God
(So my untruth had not provok'd him to it)   100
The King had cut off my head with my brother's.
What, are there no posts dispatch'd for Ireland?
How shall we do for money for these wars?
Come, sister—cousin I would say—pray pardon me.—
Go, fellow, get thee home, provide some carts   105
And bring away the armor that is there.   [*Exit Servingman.*]
Gentlemen, will you go muster men? If I
Know how or which way to order these affairs,
Thus thrust disorderly into my hands,
Never believe me. Both are my kinsmen.   110
Th' one is my sovereign, whom both my oath
And duty bids defend; t' other again
Is my kinsman, whom the King hath wrong'd,
Whom conscience and my kinred bids to right.
Well, somewhat we must do. Come, cousin, I'll   115
Dispose of you.
Gentlemen, go muster up your men,
And meet me presently at Berkeley Castle.
I should to Plashy too,
But time will not permit. All is uneven,   120
And everything is left at six and seven.   *Exeunt Duke, Queen.*

BUSHY   The wind sits fair for news to go for Ireland,
But none returns. For us to levy power
Proportionable to the enemy
Is all unpossible.   125

GREEN   Besides, our nearness to the King in love
Is near the hate of those love not the King.

BAGOT   And that's the wavering commons; for their love
Lies in their purses, and whoso empties them,
By so much fills their hearts with deadly hate.   130

---

97. **God for his mercy!:** "I pray God to be merciful!" 100. **So...to it:** provided that no disloyalty on my part had incited him to such an act. 101. **my brother's:** the Duke of Gloucester's. 104. **sister:** York is thinking of the Duchess of Gloucester. 114. **kinred:** kindred, kinship. 115. **somewhat:** something (T.P.). 119. **to:** go to. 120–21. **uneven:** in disorder. —**at six and seven:** at sixes and sevens; in a state of utter confusion. 123. **power:** forces, troops. 126–27. **our nearness, etc.:** The fact that we are close friends with the King exposes us to the hatred of those who do not love him.

BUSHY   Wherein the King stands generally condemn'd.

BAGOT   If judgment lie in them, then so do we,
               Because we ever have been near the King.

GREEN   Well, I will for refuge straight to Bristow Castle.
               The Earl of Wiltshire is already there.   135

BUSHY   Thither will I with you; for little office
               The hateful commons will perform for us,
               Except like curs to tear us all to pieces.
               Will you go along with us?

BAGOT   No; I will to Ireland to his Majesty.   140
               Farewell. If heart's presages be not vain,
               We three here part that ne'er shall meet again.

BUSHY   That's as York thrives to beat back Bolingbroke.

GREEN   Alas, poor Duke! The task he undertakes
               Is numb'ring sands and drinking oceans dry.   145
               Where one on his side fights, thousands will fly.

BAGOT   Farewell at once—for once, for all, and ever.

BUSHY   Well, we may meet again.

BAGOT   I fear me, never.   *Exeunt.*

---

131. **Wherein:** i.e., in the matter of emptying their purses. —**generally:** universally. 132. **If judgment…
we:** If the common people are to pass judgment on the King, then we shall share in their condemnation of
him. 136. **office:** service. 137. **hateful:** full of hatred. 141. **presages:** premonitions [T.P.]. 143. **That's…
Bolingbroke:** That depends on York's success in defeating Bolingbroke.

Scene III. [*The wilds in Gloucestershire.*]

Enter [Bolingbroke] the Duke of Hereford, and Northumberland.

BOLINGBROKE How far is it, my lord, to Berkeley now?†

NORTHUMBERLAND Believe me, noble lord,
        I am a stranger here in Gloucestershire.
        These high wild hills and rough uneven ways
        Draws out our miles and makes them wearisome;   5
        And yet your fair discourse hath been as sugar,
        Making the hard way sweet and delectable.
        But I bethink me what a weary way
        From Ravenspurgh to Cotshall will be found
        In Ross and Willoughby, wanting your company,   10
        Which, I protest, hath very much beguil'd
        The tediousness and process of my travel;
        But theirs is sweet'ned with the hope to have
        The present benefit which I possess;
        And hope to joy is little less in joy   15
        Than hope enjoy'd. By this the weary lords
        Shall make their way seem short, as mine hath done
        By sight of what I have, your noble company.

BOLINGBROKE Of much less value is my company
        Than your good words. But who comes here?   20

Enter Harry Percy.

NORTHUMBERLAND It is my son, young Harry Percy,
        Sent from my brother Worcester, whencesoever.
        Harry, how fares your uncle?

PERCY I had thought, my lord, to have learn'd his health of you.

NORTHUMBERLAND Why, is he not with the Queen?   25

PERCY No, my good lord; he hath forsook the court,
        Broken his staff of office, and dispers'd
        The household of the King.

NORTHUMBERLAND   What was his reason?

ACT II. SCENE III.
9. **Cotshall:** Cotswold in Gloucestershire. 10. **In:** by [T.P.]. 12. **The tediousness and process:** the tedious course. 15–16. **hope…enjoy'd:** hope to enjoy possession of anything is hardly less joyful than the possession of what one hoped for. 22. **whencesoever:** from somewhere or other.

†   In all three versions a night-time and outdoor scene, although *Bard* necessarily relies on stage lighting for the effect. Bolingbroke's soldiers in *Kings* are numerous and menacing.

	He was not so resolv'd when last we spake together.	
Percy	Because your lordship was proclaimed traitor.	30
	But he, my lord, is gone to Ravenspurgh	
	To offer service to the Duke of Hereford;	
	And sent me over by Berkeley to discover	
	What power the Duke of York had levied there;	
	Then with directions to repair to Ravenspurgh.	35

Northumberland Have you forgot the Duke of Hereford, boy?

Percy No, my good lord, for that is not forgot
Which ne'er I did remember. To my knowledge,
I never in my life did look on him.

Northumberland Then learn to know him now. This is the Duke. 40

Percy My gracious lord, I tender you my service,
Such as it is, being tender, raw, and young;
Which elder days shall ripen and confirm
To more approved service and desert.

Bolingbroke I thank thee, gentle Percy; and be sure 45
I count myself in nothing else so happy
As in a soul rememb'ring my good friends;
And, as my fortune ripens with thy love,
It shall be still thy true love's recompense.
My heart this covenant makes, my hand thus seals it. 50

Northumberland How far is it to Berkeley? and what stir
Keeps good old York there with his men of war?

Percy There stands the castle by yon tuft of trees,
Mann'd with three hundred men, as I have heard;
And in it are the Lords of York, Berkeley, and Seymour, 55
None else of name and noble estimate.

Enter Ross and Willoughby.

Northumberland Here come the Lords of Ross and Willoughby,
Bloody with spurring, fiery red with haste.

Bolingbroke Welcome, my lords. I wot your love pursues
A banish'd traitor. All my treasury 60
Is yet but unfelt thanks, which, more enrich'd,
Shall be your love and labor's recompense.

---

34. **power:** troops. 41. **tender:** offer [T.P.]. 42–44. **tender:** raw, and young. Hotspur was, in fact, about thirty-five years of age at this time (1399). —**confirm:** strengthen. 49. **still:** constantly. 52. **men of war:** soldiers. 56. **estimate:** estimation, repute. 59. **wot:** know. 60–62. **All my treasury... recompense:** All that I yet have with which to reward your love is thanks, but when my treasury is richer, my whole store shall be the recompense of your devoted service.

ROSS   Your presence makes us rich, most noble lord.

WILLOUGHBY   And far surmounts our labor to attain it.

BOLINGBROKE   Evermore thanks, the exchequer of the poor,   65
                Which, till my infant fortune comes to years,
                Stands for my bounty. But who comes here?

                           Enter Berkeley.

NORTHUMBERLAND It is my Lord of Berkeley, as I guess.†

BERKELEY   My Lord of Hereford, my message is to you.

BOLINGBROKE   My lord, my answer is—"to Lancaster";   70
                And I am come to seek that name in England;
                And I must find that title in your tongue
                Before I make reply to aught you say.

BERKELEY   Mistake me not, my lord. 'Tis not my meaning
                To rase one title of your honor out.   75
                To you, my lord, I come (what lord you will)
                From the most gracious Regent of this land,
                The Duke of York, to know what pricks you on
                To take advantage of the absent time
                And fright our native peace with self-born arms.   80

                           Enter York [attended].

BOLINGBROKE   I shall not need transport my words by you;
                Here comes his Grace in person. My noble uncle! [*Kneels.*]

YORK   Show me thy humble heart, and not thy knee,
                Whose duty is deceivable and false.

BOLINGBROKE   My gracious uncle!   85

YORK   Tut, tut!
                Grace me no grace, nor uncle me no uncle.
                I am no traitor's uncle, and that word "grace"
                In an ungracious mouth is but profane.
                Why have those banish'd and forbidden legs   90

---

65. **the exchequer:** Synonymous with "treasury" in line 60. 67. **Stands for my bounty:** must represent all that I can do in the way of generosity. 70. **my answer is—"to Lancaster":** My answer is "You must address me by my proper title—*Lancaster*, not Hereford." 75. **rase...out:** erase. 76. **what lord you will:** whatever title you may choose. 78. **pricks you on:** spurs you on; incites you. 79. **the absent time:** the time of King Richard's absence in Ireland. 80. **fright our native peace with self-born arms:** disturb the peace of our country with civil war. 84. **deceivable:** deceitful. 89. **ungracious:** graceless.

---

†   In the *Bard* version, Berkley and York are both brought in blindfolded; there is much grumbling and shouting from the troops—especially in an unusually long and wide shot, over their spears, to show six or seven characters gathered around Bolingbroke's tent.

Dared once to touch a dust of England's ground?
But then more why?—why have they dared to march
So many miles upon her peaceful bosom,
Frighting her pale-fac'd villages with war
And ostentation of despised arms?   95
Com'st thou because the anointed King is hence?
Why, foolish boy, the King is left behind,
And in my loyal bosom lies his power.
Were I but now lord of such hot youth
As when brave Gaunt thy father and myself   100
Rescued the Black Prince, that young Mars of men,
From forth the ranks of many thousand French,
O, then how quickly should this arm of mine,
Now prisoner to the palsy, chastise thee
And minister correction to thy fault!   105

BOLINGBROKE   My gracious uncle, let me know my fault;
On what condition stands it and wherein?

YORK   Even in condition of the worst degree,
In gross rebellion and detested treason.
Thou art a banish'd man; and here art come,   110
Before the expiration of thy time,
In braving arms against thy sovereign.

BOLINGBROKE   As I was banish'd, I was banish'd Hereford;
But as I come, I come for Lancaster.
And, noble uncle, I beseech your Grace   115
Look on my wrongs with an indifferent eye.
You are my father, for methinks in you
I see old Gaunt alive. O, then, my father,
Will you permit that I shall stand condemn'd
A wandering vagabond, my rights and royalties   120
Pluck'd from my arms perforce, and given away
To upstart unthrifts? Wherefore was I born?
If that my cousin king be King of England,
It must be granted I am Duke of Lancaster.

---

92. **But then more why?:** But another question follows for you to answer—and a more emphatic one. 95. **ostentation:** defiant display. **—despised:** despicable, odious. 101. **The Black Prince:** Edward, father of Richard II, and eldest son of Edward III. The Prince died in 1376, and the King in 1377, to be succeeded by his ten-year-old grandson, Richard. 104. **palsy:** paralysis. 107. **On what condition stands it and wherein?:** On what trait of character is it based, and in what does it consist? 108. **Even in condition of the worst degree:** Your fault consists in an act that is faulty in the worst possible degree. 109. **detested:** detestable. 112. **braving:** defiant. 114. **for Lancaster:** as legal claimant of the dukedon of Lancaster. 116. **indifferent:** impartial. 120. **royalties:** privileges conferred by royal grant. 122–24. **unthrifts:** spendthrifts, prodigals. **—Wherefore was I born?** "To what purpose serves birth and lineal succession? I am duke of Lancaster by the same right of birth as the king is king of England."

	You have a son, Aumerle, my noble cousin.	125
	Had you first died, and he been thus trod down,	
	He should have found his uncle Gaunt a father	
	To rouse his wrongs and chase them to the bay.	
	I am denied to sue my livery here,	
	And yet my letters patents give me leave.	130
	My father's goods are all distrain'd and sold;	
	And these, and all, are all amiss employ'd.	
	What would you have me do? I am a subject,	
	And I challenge law. Attorneys are denied me,	
	And therefore personally I lay my claim	135
	To my inheritance of free descent.	

NORTHUMBERLAND The noble Duke hath been too much abus'd.

ROSS It stands your Grace upon to do him right.

WILLOUGHBY Base men by his endowments are made great.

YORK My lords of England, let me tell you this: 140
I have had feeling of my cousin's wrongs,
And labor'd all I could to do him right;
But in this kind to come, in braving arms,
Be his own carver and cut out his way
To find out right with wrong—it may not be; 145
And you that do abet him in this kind
Cherish rebellion and are rebels all.

NORTHUMBERLAND The noble Duke hath sworn his coming is
But for his own; and for the right of that
We all have strongly sworn to give him aid; 150
And let him never see joy that breaks that oath!

YORK Well, well, I see the issue of these arms.
I cannot mend it, I must needs confess,
Because my power is weak and all ill left;
But if I could, by him that gave me life, 155
I would attach you all and make you stoop
Unto the sovereign mercy of the King;
But since I cannot, be it known to you

126. **first:** before him. 127. **should:** would certainly. 128. **To rouse...bay:** A figure from hunting. His wrongs would have been called to account and forced to stand on the defensive. 129. **denied:** refused my right. 131. **distrain'd:** seized by writ. 132. **amiss employ'd:** put to a bad use. 134. **I challenge law:** I claim my legal rights. 136. **of free descent:** which comes to me by direct and legitimate descent. 138. **It stands your Grace upon:** It is incumbent on your Grace 139. **Base:** low in rank. **—endowments:** the revenue from his lands. 143. **in this kind:** in this manner. 144. **be his own carver:** follow his own wishes—literally, serve himself at table. 145. **with wrong:** by acting wrongfully. **—it may not be:** cannot be permitted. 146. **in this kind:** in this course of action. 154. **my power...left:** my armed force is weak and left altogether ill-furnished with equipments. 156. **attach:** arrest. 159. **neuter:** neutral.

I do remain as neuter. So fare you well—
Unless you please to enter in the castle   160
And there repose you for this night.

BOLINGBROKE   An offer, uncle, that we will accept;
But we must win your Grace to go with us
To Bristow Castle, which they say is held
By Bushy, Bagot, and their complices,   165
The caterpillars of the commonwealth,
Which I have sworn to weed and pluck away.

YORK   It may be I will go with you; but yet I'll pause,
For I am loath to break our country's laws.
Nor friends nor foes, to me welcome you are.   170
Things past redress are now with me past care.   *Exeunt.*

Scene IV. [*A camp in Wales.*]

Enter Earl of Salisbury and a Welsh Captain.†

WELSH   My Lord of Salisbury, we have stay'd ten days
And hardly kept our countrymen together,
And yet we hear no tidings from the King.
Therefore we will disperse ourselves. Farewell.

SALISBURY   Stay yet another day, thou trusty Welshman.   5
The King reposeth all his confidence in thee.

WELSH   'Tis thought the King is dead. We will not stay.
The bay trees in our country all are wither'd,
And meteors fright the fixed stars of heaven;
The pale-fac'd moon looks bloody on the earth,   10
And lean-look'd prophets whisper fearful change;
Rich men look sad, and ruffians dance and leap—
The one in fear to lose what they enjoy,
The other to enjoy by rage and war.

163–64. **win:** induce. —**Bristow:** Bristol. 165. **complices:** accomplices. 166. **caterpillars:** the regular term for "parasites" or persons who enrich themselves at others' expense—especially for corrupt officials. 170. **Nor...welcome you are:** I welcome you as neutrals—neither friends nor foes.

Act II. scene IV.
2. **hardly:** with difficulty. 11. **lean-look'd:** lean-visaged. 13–14. **they enjoy:** they possess. —**to enjoy:** in hope to gain possessions. —**rage:** tumult.

---

†   *Kings* cuts this scene. *BBC* gives us only the seventeen-line dialogue between Salisbury and the Welsh captain, but not Salisbury's brief soliloquy. *Bard* (which seems committed to filming whatever *BBC* did not) cuts the dialogue, but gives us the soliloquy, now spoken, from inside a window by a character who will be identified later as Surrey and was earlier seen as the Marshall in the tournament scene. (Historically, Surrey did in fact act as marshal at that time.)

These signs forerun the death or fall of kings.   15
Farewell. Our countrymen are gone and fled,
As well assur'd Richard their king is dead.   *Exit.*

SALISBURY   Ah, Richard! with the eyes of heavy mind,
I see thy glory, like a shooting star,
Fall to the base earth from the firmament.   20
Thy sun sets weeping in the lowly West,
Witnessing storms to come, woe, and unrest;
Thy friends are fled to wait upon thy foes,
And crossly to thy good all fortune goes.   *Exit.*

ACT III

Scene I. [*Bolingbroke's camp at Bristol.*]

*Enter Bolingbroke Duke of Hereford, York, Northumberland, Ross, Percy, Willoughby,
with Bushy and Green prisoners.*

BOLINGBROKE   Bring forth these men.†
Bushy and Green, I will not vex your souls
(Since presently your souls must part your bodies)
With too much urging your pernicious lives,
For 'twere no charity; yet, to wash your blood   5
From off my hands, here in the view of men
I will unfold some causes of your deaths.
You have misled a prince, a royal king,
A happy gentleman in blood and lineaments,

---

17. **As:** as being. 18. **heavy:** sorrowful. 20. **base:** low-lying. 22. **Witnessing:** signifying. 23. **to wait upon:** to offer allegiance to. 24. **crossly:** contrariwise.

ACT III. SCENE I.
3. **presently:** immediately. —**part:** depart from. 4. **With too much urging:** by unduly emphasizing. 5. **charity:** kindness. 7. **unfold:** disclose (T. P.). 9. **happy:** fortunate. —**blood:** race, descent.

---

†   *BBC* has Bolingbroke outdoors, seated at a table with York as if he were sharing his authority, although when York starts to object to the condemnation of Bushy and Green, he is ignored. Two chopping sounds follow shortly after the favorites are taken off. *Kings* has a similar scene, but with Bolingbroke alone at a table—seemingly the same one used in 1.1 and 1.4—with Bushy and Green kneeling before it. The single camera remains fixed, showing us their backs, although we see their faces briefly when they turn to one another. The shot moves up only when Bolingbroke stands. Again we have the sound of the off-screen beheadings. *Bard* is much the most violent, the half-dressed Bushy and Green seem to have been tortured and are roughly handled by Willoughby and Exton (again for Ross). Bolingbroke in great anger strikes Bushy, who spits at him; the off-camera screams and groans indicate a much less humane execution.

By you unhappied and disfigured clean.   10
You have in manner with your sinful hours
Made a divorce betwixt his queen and him,
Broke the possession of a royal bed,
And stain'd the beauty of a fair queen's cheeks
With tears drawn from her eyes by your foul wrongs.   15
Myself—a prince by fortune of my birth,
Near to the King in blood, and near in love
Till you did make him misinterpret me—
Have stoop'd my neck under your injuries
And sigh'd my English breath in foreign clouds,   20
Eating the bitter bread of banishment,
Whilst you have fed upon my signories,
Dispark'd my parks and fell'd my forest woods,
From my own windows torn my household coat,
Ras'd out my imprese, leaving me no sign,   25
Save men's opinions and my living blood,
To show the world I am a gentleman.
This and much more, much more than twice all this,
Condemns you to the death. See them delivered over
To execution and the hand of death.   30

BUSHY   More welcome is the stroke of death to me
                 Than Bolingbroke to England. Lords, farewell.

GREEN   My comfort is that heaven will take our souls
                 And plague injustice with the pains of hell.

BOLINGBROKE My Lord Northumberland, see them dispatch'd.   35
                 [Exeunt Northumberland and others, with the prisoners.]
                 Uncle, you say the Queen is at your house.
                 For God's sake, fairly let her be entreated.
                 Tell her I send to her my kind commends;
                 Take special care my greetings be delivered.

YORK   A gentleman of mine I have dispatch'd   40
                 With letters of your love to her at large.

---

11. **in manner:** in a way; so to speak. The phrase modifies "made a divorce." —**with your sinful hours:** by your association with him in riotous living. 13. **Broke:** interrupted. There is no historical basis for the assertion that Bushy and Green had thus estranged the King and Queen, 19. **stoop'd my neck:** submitted without resistance. 20. **foreign clouds:** clouds of breath exhaled in foreign climes. 22. **my signiories:** the lands which I possessed as their lord. 23. **Dispark'd:** To *dispark* is a legal term, and signifies, to divest a park, constituted by royal grant or prescription, of its name and character, by destroying the enclosures of such a park. 24. **my household coat:** the coat of arms of my family, displayed in the painted windows. 25. **Ras'd out:** erased. —**imprese:** a heraldic device or emblem, with a motto. 26. **my living blood:** myself, so long as I lived. 37. **entreated:** treated. 38. **commends:** regards. 41. **at large:** in full.

BOLINGBROKE Thanks, gentle uncle. Come, lords, away,
To fight with Glendower and his complices.
Awhile to work, and after holiday.   *Exeunt.*

Scene II. [*The coast of Wales. A castle in view.*]

Drums. Flourish and Colors. Enter the King, Aumerle, [the Bishop of] Carlisle, and Soldiers.

KING   Barkloughly Castle call they this at hand?

AUMERLE   Yea, my lord. How brooks your Grace the air
After your late tossing on the breaking seas?

KING   Needs must I like it well. I weep for joy
To stand upon my kingdom once again.†   5
Dear earth, I do salute thee with my hand,
Though rebels wound thee with their horses' hoofs.
As a long-parted mother with her child
Plays fondly with her tears and smiles in meeting,
So weeping, smiling, greet I thee, my earth,   10
And do thee favors with my royal hands.
Feed not thy sovereign's foe, my gentle earth,
Nor with thy sweets comfort his ravenous sense;
But let thy spiders that suck up thy venom,
And heavy-gaited toads, lie in their way,   15
Doing annoyance to the treacherous feet
Which with usurping steps do trample thee.
Yield stinging nettles to mine enemies;
And when they from thy bosom pluck a flower,
Guard it, I pray thee, with a lurking adder   20
Whose double tongue may with a mortal touch

---

43. **Glendower:** Owen Glendower, who had been a squire in attendance on King Richard. He has escaped to Wales. He plays an important part in *1 Henry IV.* —**complices:** accomplices. 44. **after:** afterwards.

ACT III. SCENE II.

1. **Barkloughly Castle:** *Harlech* in North Wales, where Richard landed (on his return from Ireland) late in July, 1399. 2. **How brooks your Grace the air?** How does your Majesty like the air? How does it agree with you? 8. **a long-parted mother with her child:** a mother long parted from her child. 9. **Fondly:** *Fondly* here suggest both "foolishly" and "affectionately" [T.P.]. 12. **do thee favors:** i.e., in my gestures of greeting. 13. **comfort his ravenous sense:** satisfy his voracious appetite. 16. **annoyance:** injury, harm. 20. **adder:** a poisonous snake [T.P.]. 21. **mortal:** fatal [T.P.].

---

†   *BBC* has a wooden portal at the back of the scene that suggests the dock at which Richard has just disembarked. *Bard,* like *BBC,* makes this night scene; as often happens, the background is blacked out, and we see only a small portion of the playing area—in this case, the bottom of one of the staircases and the platform stage around it.

Throw death upon thy sovereign's enemies.
Mock not my senseless conjuration, lords.
This earth shall have a feeling, and these stones
Prove armed soldiers ere her native king   25
Shall falter under foul rebellion's arms.

CARLISLE   Fear not, my lord. That Power that made you king
Hath power to keep you king in spite of all.
The means that heaven yields must be embrac'd,
And not neglected; else, if heaven would,   30
And we will not, heaven's offer we refuse,
The proffered means of succour and redress.

AUMERLE   He means, my lord, that we are too remiss,
Whilst Bolingbroke, through our security,
Grows strong and great in substance and in power.   35

KING   Discomfortable cousin! know'st thou not
That when the searching eye of heaven is hid
Behind the globe, that lights the lower world,
Then thieves and robbers range abroad unseen
In murthers and in outrage boldly here;   40
But when from under this terrestrial ball
He fires the proud tops of the Eastern pines
And darts his light through every guilty hole,
Then murthers, treasons, and detested sins,
The cloak of night being pluck'd from off their backs,   45
Stand bare and naked, trembling at themselves?
So when this thief, this traitor Bolingbroke,
Who all this while hath revell'd in the night
Whilst we were wand'ring with the Antipodes,
Shall see us rising in our throne, the East,   50
His treasons will sit blushing in his face,
Not able to endure the sight of day,
But self-affrighted tremble at his sin.
Not all the water in the rough rude sea
Can wash the balm off from an anointed king.   55

---

22. **Throw:** inflict. 23. **Mock not my senseless conjuration:** Do not ridicule my adjuration (my solemn appeal), as being addressed to the earth, which has no sense of hearing or feeling. 25. **prove:** shall become [T.P.]. 29. **yields:** grants, affords. 34. **security:** remissness, negligence. 35. **in substance and in power:** in resources and in troops. 36. **Discomfortable:** Used in an active sense: "discomforting," "discouraging." 38. **the globe:** this earth. The earth is being thought of as the center of the universe, around which the sun "the searching eye of heaven," revolves [T.P.]. —**that:** The antecedent is *eye of heaven*. 41. **terrestrial ball:** the earth [T.P.]. 42. **fires:** lights, literally, sets on fire [T.P.]. 43. **guilty hole:** hiding place of the guilty. 44. **detested:** detestable. 47. **thief:** robber. A stronger word than in modern usage. 49. **we:** I, the King. —**the Antipodes:** those who live on the other side of the globe [T.P.]. 55. **the balm:** the holy oil with which the king is anointed at his coronation.

The breath of worldly men cannot depose
The deputy elected by the Lord.
For every man that Bolingbroke hath press'd
To lift shrewd steel against our golden crown,
God for his Richard hath in heavenly pay   60
A glorious angel. Then, if angels fight,
Weak men must fall; for heaven still guards the right.

Enter Salisbury.

Welcome, my lord. How far off lies your power?

SALISBURY   Nor near nor farther off, my gracious lord,
Than this weak arm. Discomfort guides my tongue   65
And bids me speak of nothing but despair.
One day too late, I fear me, noble lord,
Hath clouded all thy happy days on earth.
O, call back yesterday, bid time return,
And thou shalt have twelve thousand fighting men!   70
Today, today, unhappy day too late,
O'erthrows thy joys, friends, fortune, and thy state;
For all the Welshmen, hearing thou wert dead,
Are gone to Bolingbroke, dispers'd, and fled.

AUMERLE   Comfort, my liege. Why looks your Grace so pale?   75

KING   But now the blood of twenty thousand men
Did triumph in my face, and they are fled;
And, till so much blood thither come again,
Have I not reason to look pale and dead?
All souls that will be safe, fly from my side;   80
For time hath set a blot upon my pride.

AUMERLE   Comfort, my liege. Remember who you are.

KING   I had forgot myself. Am I not King?
Awake, thou coward majesty! thou sleepest.
Is not the King's name twenty thousand names?   85
Arm, arm, my name! A puny subject strikes
At thy great glory. Look not to the ground,
Ye favorites of a king. Are we not high?
High be our thoughts. I know my uncle York
Hath power enough to serve our turn. But who comes here? 90

---

56. **worldly men:** men of this world. 58. **press'd:** impressed; enlisted by conscription. 59. **shrewd:** harmful. 62. **still:** ever, always. 63. **power:** army. 64. **Nor...nor:** neither...nor. —**near:** nearer. 65. **Discomfort:** discouragement. 72. **state:** majesty; royal authority. 77. **triumph:** glow triumphantly. 84. **coward:** cowardly. 90. **power:** troops.

Enter Scroop.

SCROOP   More health and happiness betide my liege
          Than can my care-tun'd tongue deliver him!

KING   Mine ear is open and my heart prepar'd.
          The worst is worldly loss thou canst unfold.
          Say, is my kingdom lost? Why, 'twas my care;   95
          And what loss is it to be rid of care?
          Strives Bolingbroke to be as great as we?
          Greater he shall not be; if he serve God,
          We'll serve him too, and be his fellow so.
          Revolt our subjects? That we cannot mend;   100
          They break their faith to God as well as us.
          Cry woe, destruction, ruin, and decay:
          The worst is death, and death will have his day.

SCROOP   Glad am I that your Highness is so arm'd
          To bear the tidings of calamity.   105
          Like an unseasonable stormy day
          Which makes the silver rivers drown their shores
          As if the world were all dissolv'd to tears,
          So high above his limits swells the rage
          Of Bolingbroke, covering your fearful land   110
          With hard bright steel, and hearts harder than steel.
          White-beards have arm'd their thin and hairless scalps
          Against thy majesty. Boys with women's voices
          Strive to speak big, and clap their female joints
          In stiff unwieldy arms against thy crown.   115
          Thy very beadsmen learn to bend their bows
          Of double-fatal yew against thy state.
          Yea, distaff-women manage rusty bills
          Against thy seat. Both young and old rebel,
          And all goes worse than I have power to tell.   120

KING   Too well, too well thou tell'st a tale so ill.
          Where is the Earl of Wiltshire? Where is Bagot?

---

92. **care-tun'd:** tuned to sounds of sorrow. **—deliver him:** report to him. 94. **The worst...unfold:** The worst which you can disclose is loss of worldly possessions. 95. **my care:** the source of all my trouble and anxiety. 97. **we:** The "royal *we*"—"I the King." 99. **fellow:** equal [T.P.]. 100. **cannot mend:** cannot remedy; cannot help. 102. **Cry:** proclaim. 109. **his:** its. 112. **arm'd:** i.e., with helmets. **—thin:** scanty-haired. 114–15. **clap...In:** hurriedly thrust their limbs—weak as those of women—into. 116. **beadsmen:** aged pensioners, whose duty was to pray for their benefactors. 117. **double-fatal:** because its leaves and berries are poisonous and its wood is used for deadly weapons (bows). **—state:** royal majesty. 118–19. **distaff-women:** women, who should wield nothing more dangerous than the distaff—a staff used in spinning, and regarded as the characteristic weapon of women. **—manage:** wield. **—bills:** halberds, pikes. **—seat:** throne.

What is become of Bushy? Where is Green?
That they have let the dangerous enemy
Measure our confines with such peaceful steps?   125
If we prevail, their heads shall pay for it.
I warrant they have made peace with Bolingbroke.

SCROOP   Peace have they made with him indeed, my lord.

KING   O villains, vipers, damn'd without redemption!
Dogs easily won to fawn on any man!   130
Snakes in my heart-blood warm'd that sting my heart!
Three Judases, each one thrice worse than Judas!
Would they make peace? Terrible hell make war
Upon their spotted souls for this offence!

SCROOP   Sweet love, I see, changing his property,   135
Turns to the sourest and most deadly hate.
Again uncurse their souls. Their peace is made
With heads, and not with hands. Those whom you curse
Have felt the worst of death's destroying wound
And lie full low, grav'd in the hollow ground.   140

AUMERLE   Is Bushy, Green, and the Earl of Wiltshire dead?

SCROOP   Ay, all of them at Bristow lost their heads.

AUMERLE   Where is the Duke my father with his power?

KING   No matter where. Of comfort no man speak!
Let's talk of graves, of worms, and epitaphs,   145
Make dust our paper, and with rainy eyes
Write sorrow on the bosom of the earth.
Let's choose executors and talk of wills.
And yet not so—for what can we bequeath,
Save our deposed bodies to the ground?   150
Our lands, our lives, and all are Bolingbroke's,
And nothing can we call our own but death
And that small model of the barren earth
Which serves as paste and cover to our bones.
For God's sake let us sit upon the ground   155
And tell sad stories of the death of kings!
How some have been depos'd, some slain in war,

---

125. **measure:** traverse. —**peaceful:** unopposed. 128. **Peace have they made with him indeed:** because he has put them to death—which is peace indeed! 134. **spotted:** i.e., with the venom of treason. 135. **changing his property:** when it changes from its essential quality. 138. **with hands:** by hands raised in submission. 142. **Bristow:** Bristol. 153–54. **that small model of the barren earth:** that small quantity of barren earth which outlines the shape of our body as we lie in the grave. —**paste and cover:** Metaphorically, like the crust of a pastry [T.P.].

Some haunted by the ghosts they have depos'd,
Some poisoned by their wives, some sleeping kill'd—
All murthered; for within the hollow crown   160
That rounds the mortal temples of a king
Keeps Death his court; and there the antic sits,
Scoffing his state and grinning at his pomp;
Allowing him a breath, a little scene,
To monarchize, be fear'd, and kill with looks;   165
Infusing him with self and vain conceit,
As if this flesh which walls about our life
Were brass impregnable; and humor'd thus,
Comes at the last, and with a little pin
Bores through his castle wall, and farewell king!   170
Cover your heads, and mock not flesh and blood
With solemn reverence. Throw away respect,
Tradition, form, and ceremonious duty;
For you have but mistook me all this while.
I live with bread like you, feel want, taste grief,   175
Need friends. Subjected thus,
How can you say to me I am a king?

CARLISLE   My lord, wise men ne'er sit and wail their woes,
But presently prevent the ways to wail.
To fear the foe, since fear oppresseth strength,   180
Gives, in your weakness, strength unto your foe,
And so your follies fight against yourself.
Fear, and be slain—no worse can come to fight;
And fight and die is death destroying death,
Where fearing dying pays death servile breath.   185

AUMERLE   My father hath a power. Inquire of him,
And learn to make a body of a limb.

KING   Thou chid'st me well. Proud Bolingbroke, I come

---

158. **the ghosts they have depos'd:** the ghosts of the kings whom they have deposed. 161. **rounds:** encircles [T.P.]. 162. **the antic:** the grotesque fool (jester), who makes sport of him. 163. **scoffing his state:** ridiculing his royal splendor. —**pomp:** magnificence. 164–65. **a little scene To monarchize:** a short time, like a scene in a play, in which to act the part of a king. 166. **self and vain conceit:** "a foolish and unwarranted idea about himself," as if he were immortal. 168. **humor'd thus:** when he (the king) has been thus indulged in his delusion. 169. **Comes:** he (Death) comes. 170. **his castle wall:** the wall of his mortal body. 171. **Cover your heads:** It was customary to remove one's hat in the presence of the king [T.P.]. 176. **Subjected thus:** since I am thus reduced to the condition of a subject. 179. **presently:** promptly, instantly. —**prevent the ways to wail:** cut off in advance the courses of action that lead one to lament. 180. **fear oppresseth strength:** fear crushes one's strength. 183. **to fight:** in fighting; if one fights. 185. **Where...breath:** whereas to die *in fear* is to yield cowardly and slavish obedience to death's commands. 186. **a power:** a troop of soldiery. —**of:** concerning. 187. **to make a body of a limb:** to make a whole army out of a single troop.

To change blows with thee for our day of doom.
This ague fit of fear is overblown.   190
An easy task it is to win our own.
Say, Scroop, where lies our uncle with his power?
Speak sweetly, man, although thy looks be sour.

SCROOP   Men judge by the complexion of the sky
The state and inclination of the day;   195
So may you by my dull and heavy eye:
My tongue hath but a heavier tale to say.
I play the torturer, by small and small
To lengthen out the worst that must be spoken.
Your uncle York is join'd with Bolingbroke,   200
And all your Northern castles yielded up,
And all your Southern gentlemen in arms
Upon his party.

KING   Thou hast said enough.
[*To Aumerle*] Beshrew thee, cousin, which didst lead me forth
Of that sweet way I was in to despair!   205
What say you now? What comfort have we now?
By heaven, I'll hate him everlastingly
That bids me be of comfort any more.
Go to Flint Castle. There I'll pine away;
A king, woe's slave, shall kingly woe obey.   210
That power I have, discharge; and let them go
To ear the land that hath some hope to grow,
For I have none. Let no man speak again
To alter this, for counsel is but vain.

AUMERLE   My liege, one word.

KING   He does me double wrong   215
That wounds me with the flatteries of his tongue.
Discharge my followers. Let them hence away,
From Richard's night to Bolingbroke's fair day.†   *Exeunt.*

---

189. **change:** exchange. —**for...doom:** to determine which of us shall be doomed to defeat. 190. **ague fit:** a fit of fear and feverish trembling [T.P.]. 197. **heavier:** gloomier and more sorrowful. 198. **the torturer:** The allusion is to the torture of the rack. —**by small and small:** little by little. 199. **to lengthen:** in lengthening. 203. **Upon his party:** on his side. 204. **Beshrew:** literally, "curse," but always used in a mild sense. —**which:** who. 205. **Of:** from. 209. **Flint Castle:** In Wales, near Chester. 212. **To ear... grow:** to plough the soil that has some prospect of a harvest.

---

†   *Kings* ends the first of its two episodes of the play with this scene, and closes effectively with a rare full-length shot of David William as Richard alone against an empty background, despairing of his crown. The effect is undermined, however, by requiring him to hold his pose while his supporters exit behind him to the right and then the closing credits roll over him.

Scene III. [*Wales. Before Flint Castle.*]

Enter, with Drum and Colors, Bolingbroke, York, Northumberland, Attendants, [and Soldiers].

BOLINGBROKE. So that by this intelligence we learn
    The Welshmen are dispers'd, and Salisbury
    Is gone to meet the King, who lately landed
    With some few private friends upon this coast.

NORTHUMBERLAND The news is very fair and good, my lord.†   5
    Richard not far from hence hath hid his head.

YORK   It would beseem the Lord Northumberland
    To say "King Richard." Alack the heavy day
    When such a sacred king should hide his head!

NORTHUMBERLAND Your Grace mistakes. Only to be brief,   10
    Left I his title out.

YORK   The time hath been,
    Would you have been so brief with him, he would
    Have been so brief with you to shorten you,
    For taking so the head, your whole head's length.

BOLINGBROKE Mistake not, uncle, further than you should.   15

YORK   Take not, good cousin, further than you should,
    Lest you mistake. The heavens are over our heads.

BOLINGBROKE I know it, uncle, and oppose not myself
    Against their will. But who comes here?

Enter Percy.

    Welcome, Harry. What, will not this castle yield?   20

PERCY   The castle royally is mann'd, my lord,
    Against thy entrance.

ACT III. SCENE III.
1. **intelligence:** information. 13. **to:** as to. 14. **For taking so the head:** for being so hasty as to take away his title. 15. **Mistake…should:** Do not willfully misinterpret Northumberland's language. 16. **cousin:** nephew. 17. **mistake:** *mis*-take: take that to which you have no claim.

---

†   The text requires that Richard and Bolingbroke be in sight of one another, but out of earshot, thus requiring Northumberland to shuttle back and forth between them twice. *BBC*, with the largest resources and the most mobile camera, gives us dramatically steep shots downward from Richard, perhaps twenty feet up on the walls of Flint Castle, and upward from Northumberland below in the "base court." The camera moves inside the castle to allow Derek Jacobi to recite the Phaeton speech (lines 179-84) while descending an interior staircase.

BOLINGBROKE Royally?
             Why, it contains no king?

PERCY   Yes, my good lord,
             It doth contain a king. King Richard lies   25
             Within the limits of yon lime and stone;
             And with him are the Lord Aumerle, Lord Salisbury,
             Sir Stephen Scroop, besides a clergyman
             Of holy reverence—who, I cannot learn.

NORTHUMBERLAND O, belike it is the Bishop of Carlisle.   30

BOLINGBROKE Noble lords,
             Go to the rude ribs of that ancient castle;
             Through brazen trumpet send the breath of parley
             Into his ruin'd ears, and thus deliver:
             Henry Bolingbroke   35
             On both his knees doth kiss King Richard's hand
             And sends allegiance and true faith of heart
             To his most royal person; hither come
             Even at his feet to lay my arms and power,
             Provided that my banishment repeal'd   40
             And lands restor'd again be freely granted.
             If not, I'll use the advantage of my power,
             And lay the summer's dust with show'rs of blood
             Rain'd from the wounds of slaughtered Englishmen;
             The which, how far off from the mind of Bolingbroke   45
             It is, such crimson tempest should bedrench
             The fresh green lap of fair King Richard's land,
             My stooping duty tenderly shall show.
             Go signify as much, while here we march
             Upon the grassy carpet of this plain.   50
             Let's march without the noise of threat'ning drum,
             That from this castle's tattered battlements
             Our fair appointments may be well perus'd.
             Methinks King Richard and myself should meet
             With no less terror than the elements   55
             Of fire and water when their thund'ring shock
             At meeting tears the cloudy cheeks of heaven.
             Be he the fire, I'll be the yielding water;

30. **belike:** probably, doubtless. 32. **the rude ribs:** the rough walls. 33. **the breath of parley:** a trumpet signal for a conference. 34. **deliver:** proclaim. 42. **the advantage of my power:** my superiority in military forces. 48. **My stooping duty:** my reverential obeisance. 53. **our fair appointments:** our gallant outfit. —**perus'd:** scanned. 55–57. **the elements…heaven:** One old scientific explanation of thunder was that it is caused by a clash between the contrary elements of fire and water. A fiery vapor bursts forth from a watery cloud in which it has been confined.

The rage be his, whilst on the earth I rain
My waters—on the earth, and not on him.   60
March on, and mark King Richard how he looks.

Parle without, and answer within; then a flourish.
Enter, on the walls, [King] Richard, [the Bishop of] Carlisle, Aumerle, Scroop, Salisbury.

See, see, King Richard doth himself appear,
As doth the blushing discontented sun
From out the fiery portal of the East
When he perceives the envious clouds are bent   65
To dim his glory and to stain the track
Of his bright passage to the Occident.

YORK   Yet looks he like a king. Behold, his eye,
As bright as is the eagle's, lightens forth
Controlling majesty. Alack, alack, for woe,   70
That any harm should stain so fair a show!

KING   [*to Northumberland*] We are amaz'd; and thus long have we stood†
To watch the fearful bending of thy knee,
Because we thought ourself thy lawful king.
And if we be, how dare thy joints forget   75
To pay their awful duty to our presence?
If we be not, show us the hand of God
That hath dismiss'd us from our stewardship;
For well we know no hand of blood and bone
Can gripe the sacred handle of our sceptre,   80
Unless he do profane, steal, or usurp.
And though you think that all, as you have done,
Have torn their souls by turning them from us

61.S.D. *Parle:* trumpet call for a parley. —*on the walls:* They enter on the upper stage. 65. **envious:** spiteful, hostile. —**are bent:** intend; are determined. 69–70. **lightens forth...majesty:** flashes with authoritative majesty. 71. **should stain so fair a show!** should deface so beautiful an aspect! 72–73. **amaz'd:** in a maze. A strong word for utter confusion of mind. —**stood...knee:** stood silent waiting to see you bend your knee in reverence. 76. **awful duty:** reverential homage. 77. **the hand of God:** God's signature. 80. **gripe:** seize [T.P.]. 81. **Unless...usurp:** without incurring the guilt of sacrilege, robbery, or usurpation. 83. **torn their souls:** torn their souls asunder. —**turning them from:** turning themselves away from.

---

†   *Kings* gives us a castle wall no more than seven or eight feet high; Northumberland seems to be standing on a staircase to Richard's right, just a step or two lower. *Bard*, like the other two versions, makes this a night time scene, which here requires some intricate stage lighting, with Bolingbroke's party in darkness, but lit upward through a filter that suggests the glow of a campfire. Richard, as in *Kings*, is seven or eight feet above the main stage on the bare platform that runs the width of the set. The lack of space compromises the sense of Northumberland moving back and forth between the antagonists. Bolingbroke is clearly visible and no more than five feet or so behind Northumberland when Richard claims "For yonder I think he stands."

And we are barren and bereft of friends,
Yet know, my master, God omnipotent,   85
Is mustering in his clouds on our behalf
Armies of pestilence, and they shall strike
Your children yet unborn and unbegot
That lift your vassal hands against my head
And threat the glory of my precious crown.   90
Tell Bolingbroke, for yon methinks he stands,
That every stride he makes upon my land
Is dangerous treason. He is come to open
The purple testament of bleeding war.
But ere the crown he looks for live in peace,   95
Ten thousand bloody crowns of mothers' sons
Shall ill become the flower of England's face,
Change the complexion of her maid-pale peace
To scarlet indignation, and bedew
Her pastures' grass with faithful English blood.   100

NORTHUMBERLAND The King of Heaven forbid our lord the King
Should so with civil and uncivil arms
Be rush'd upon! Thy thrice-noble cousin
Harry Bolingbroke doth humbly kiss thy hand;
And by the honourable tomb he swears   105
That stands upon your royal grandsire's bones,
And by the royalties of both your bloods
(Currents that spring from one most gracious head),
And by the buried hand of warlike Gaunt,
And by the worth and honor of himself,   110
Comprising all that may be sworn or said,
His coming hither hath no further scope
Than for his lineal royalties, and to beg
Enfranchisement immediate on his knees;
Which on thy royal party granted once,   115
His glittering arms he will commend to rust,

---

89. **That:** The antecedent is *your* (= of you). 93–94. **to open The purple testament:** *Testament* means
will: "Bolingbroke means to open War's will and lay claim to the legacy which it grants him." —**purple:**
blood-red. 96. **crowns:** heads [T.P.]. 100. **the flower of England's face:** The double meaning comes out
fully in the two lines that follow: "The blooming loveliness of the English countryside shall be stained
with the blood of her loyal sons, and the maidenly fairness of the peace which England enjoys shall be
changed to the blood-red complexion of wrath." 102. **civil and uncivil:** i.e, in civil war and barbarously
[T.P.]. 106. **your royal grandsire's:** Edward the Third's. The tomb is in Westminster Abbey. 107. **both
your bloods:** the lineage of both of you. 108. **gracious:** noble. —**head:** fountain head; source. 111.
Comprising...said: in a word, by every oath that can be sworn or uttered. 112. **hath no further scope:**
extends to no further purpose. 113. **his lineal royalties:** the hereditary rights that are his by royal grant.
114. **Enfranchisement:** release from the penalties of banishment. 115. **party:** part. 116. **commend:**
commit, hand over. 117. **barbed:** equipped with armor.

His barbed steeds to stables, and his heart
To faithful service of your Majesty.
This swears he, as he is a prince, is just;
And as I am a gentleman, I credit him.   120

KING   Northumberland, say thus the King returns:
His noble cousin is right welcome hither;
And all the number of his fair demands
Shall be accomplish'd without contradiction.
With all the gracious utterance thou hast   125
Speak to his gentle hearing kind commends.
[*To Aumerle*] We do debase ourselves, cousin, do we not,
To look so poorly and to speak so fair?
Shall we call back Northumberland and send
Defiance to the traitor, and so die?   130

AUMERLE   No, good my lord. Let's fight with gentle words
Till time lend friends, and friends their helpful swords.

KING   O God, O God! that e'er this tongue of mine
That laid the sentence of dread banishment
On yon proud man, should take it off again   135
With words of sooth! O that I were as great
As is my grief, or lesser than my name!
Or that I could forget what I have been!
Or not remember what I must be now!
Swell'st thou, proud heart? I'll give thee scope to beat,   140
Since foes have scope to beat both thee and me.

AUMERLE   Northumberland comes back from Bolingbroke.

KING   What must the King do now? Must he submit?
The King shall do it. Must he be depos'd?
The King shall be contented. Must he lose   145
The name of king? A God's name, let it go!
I'll give my jewels for a set of beads,
My gorgeous palace for a hermitage,
My gay apparel for an almsman's gown,
My figur'd goblets for a dish of wood,   150
My sceptre for a palmer's walking staff,
My subjects for a pair of carved saints,

---

119. **just:** true. 120. **I credit him:** I believe his oath. 121. **returns:** sends back in reply. 123. **demands:** requests. Not so imperative a term as in modern usage. 124. **accomplish'd:** fulfilled, granted. 125–26. **With all...kind commends:** Use your utmost courtesy in tone and words in giving him my kind regards. 128. **so poorly:** with such pitiful lack of spirit and courage. 136. **words of sooth:** words of soothing; flattering words. 137. **my name:** my title. 140. **scope:** liberty, permission. 146. **A:** in. 147. **a set of beads:** a rosary. 151. **palmer:** pilgrim .

And my large kingdom for a little grave,
A little little grave, an obscure grave;
Or I'll be buried in the king's highway, 155
Some way of common trade, where subjects' feet
May hourly trample on their sovereign's head;
For on my heart they tread now whilst I live,
And buried once, why not upon my head?
Aumerle, thou weep'st, my tender-hearted cousin! 160
We'll make foul weather with despised tears;
Our sighs and they shall lodge the summer corn
And make a dearth in this revolting land.
Or shall we play the wantons with our woes
And make some pretty match with shedding tears? 165
As thus—to drop them still upon one place
Till they have fretted us a pair of graves
Within the earth; and therein laid—there lies
Two kinsmen digg'd their graves with weeping eyes.
Would not this ill do well? Well, well, I see 170
I talk but idly, and you laugh at me.
Most mighty prince, my Lord Northumberland,
What says King Bolingbroke? Will his Majesty
Give Richard leave to live till Richard die?
You make a leg, and Bolingbroke says ay. 175

NORTHUMBERLAND My lord, in the base court he doth attend
To speak with you, may it please you to come down.

KING Down, down I come, like glist'ring Phaëton,†
Wanting the manage of unruly jades.
In the base court? Base court, where kings grow base, 180
To come at traitors' calls and do them grace!
In the base court? Come down? Down court! down king!

---

156. **trade:** traffic, passage. 159. **buried once:** once I am buried [T.P.]. 162. **lodge:** beat down. **—corn:** wheat. 163. **dearth:** famine. **—revolting:** rebellious. 164–65. **shall we play the wantons ...tears?** Shall we sport with our own sorrows and play some clever game? 167. **fretted:** To *fret* is, literally, to "eat away." 169. **digg'd:** who dug. 171. **idly:** foolishly; in a silly fashion. 175. **a leg:** a curtsy. 176. **the base court:** the lower courtyard of the castle; the outer court. 178–79. **Phaëton:** Apollo's son, who lost control of his father's sun chariot and was destroyed by Zeus to prevent his incinerating the world [T.P.]. **—Wanting the manage of:** lacking the strength to handle. **—jades:** a contemptuous term for "horses." 181. **grace:** honor.

---

† David Birney gives a rather manic reading of the Phaeton speech, running down one of the stage staircases with his cloak flapping behind him. At the end of the scene, *Bard* and *Kings* both have everyone on stage ignore Richard's "Set on towards London" until Bolingbroke endorses the order. He has clearly been taken into custody in both versions.

For night owls shriek where mounting larks should sing.

[*Exeunt from above.*]

BOLINGBROKE What says his Majesty?

NORTHUMBERLAND   Sorrow and grief of heart
Makes him speak fondly, like a frantic man.   185
Yet he is come.

[*Enter King Richard attended, below.*]

BOLINGBROKE Stand all apart
And show fair duty to his Majesty. †   *He kneels down.*
My gracious lord—

KING Fair cousin, you debase your princely knee   190
To make the base earth proud with kissing it.
Me rather had my heart might feel your love
Than my unpleas'd eye see your courtesy.
Up, cousin, up! Your heart is up, I know,
Thus high at least [*touches his own head*], although your knee be low.

BOLINGBROKE [*rises*] My gracious lord, I come but for mine own.   196

KING Your own is yours, and I am yours, and all.

BOLINGBROKE So far be mine, my most redoubted lord,
As my true service shall deserve your love.

KING Well you deserve. They well deserve to have   200
That know the strong'st and surest way to get.
Uncle, give me your hand. Nay, dry your eyes.
Tears show their love, but want their remedies.
Cousin, I am too young to be your father,
Though you are old enough to be my heir.   205
What you will have, I'll give, and willing too;
For do we must what force will have us do.
Set on towards London. Cousin, is it so?

BOLINGBROKE Yea, my good lord.

KING   Then I must not say no.   *Flourish. Exeunt.*

---

183. **night owls shriek:** An omen of disaster or death. 185. **speak fondly:** speak foolishly; talk nonsense.
—**frantic:** raving mad. 192. **Me rather had:** I had rather. 193. **courtesy:** Here the word combines two
meanings—"courtesy" and "curtsy." 197. **is yours:** for you have already taken possession of it. —**all:**
everything. 198. **So far be mine:** Be "mine" to the degree that I deserve your favor [T.P.]. —**redoubted:**
held in awe. 202. **Uncle:** He turns from Bolingbroke to York. 203. **Tears...remedies:** Tears reveal their
love for the person for whom they are shed, but they lack the power to remedy his misfortunes. 204–05.
Cousin: Addressed to Bolingbroke. —**to be my heir:** to inherit my kingdom.

---

†   The menace of Bolingbroke's supporters in *Kings* is, if anything, even greater, and his "Stand all
apart/ And show fair duty to his Majesty" has to restrain them from attacking Richard.

Scene IV. [*Langley. The Duke of York's garden.*]†

Enter the Queen with two Ladies, her Attendants.

QUEEN   What sport shall we devise here in this garden
           To drive away the heavy thought of care?

LADY   Madam, we'll play at bowls.

QUEEN   'Twill make me think the world is full of rubs
           And that my fortune runs against the bias.   5

LADY   Madam, we'll dance.

QUEEN   My legs can keep no measure in delight
           When my poor heart no measure keeps in grief.
           Therefore no dancing, girl; some other sport.

LADY   Madam, we'll tell tales.   10

QUEEN   Of sorrow or of joy?

LADY   Of either, madam.

QUEEN   Of neither, girl;
           For if of joy, being altogether wanting,
           It doth remember me the more of sorrow;
           Or if of grief, being altogether had,   15
           It adds more sorrow to my want of joy;
           For what I have I need not to repeat,
           And what I want it boots not to complain.

LADY   Madam, I'll sing.

QUEEN   'Tis well that thou hast cause;
           But thou shouldst please me better, wouldst thou weep.   20

LADY   I could weep, madam, would it do you good.

QUEEN   And I could sing, would weeping do me good,
           And never borrow any tear of thee.

           Enter a Gardener and two Servants.

ACT III. SCENE IV.
4–5. **rubs…bias:** Technical terms in bowling. A *rub* is any impediment that interferes with the course of the ball; the *bias* is the course of the ball—the "curve." 7. **no measure:** no figure (in dancing). 8. **measure:** moderation, limit. 14. **remember:** remind. 15. **had:** i.e., by me. 18. **it boots not:** it avails not; it does no good. —**complain:** lament the lack of. 20. **shouldst:** would certainly. 22. **sing:** i.e., for joy that weeping would be of any avail.

---

†   *Kings* opens with the table at which Richard had presided in the opening scene—now covered with broken dishes, cobwebs, even mice—suggesting a considerable lapse of time.

But stay, here come the gardeners.†
Let's step into the shadow of these trees.   25
My wretchedness unto a row of pins,
They will talk of state, for every one doth so
Against a change: woe is forerun with woe.

[Queen and Ladies step aside.]

GARDENER   Go bind thou up yon dangling apricocks,
Which, like unruly children, make their sire   30
Stoop with oppression of their prodigal weight.
Give some supportance to the bending twigs.
Go thou and, like an executioner,
Cut off the heads of too fast growing sprays
That look too lofty in our commonwealth.   35
All must be even in our government.
You thus employ'd, I will go root away
The noisome weeds which without profit suck
The soil's fertility from wholesome flowers.

MAN   Why should we, in the compass of a pale,   40
Keep law and form and due proportion,
Showing, as in a model, our firm estate,
When our sea-walled garden, the whole land,
Is full of weeds, her fairest flowers chok'd up,
Her fruit trees all unprun'd, her hedges ruin'd,   45
Her knots disordered, and her wholesome herbs
Swarming with caterpillars?

GARDENER   Hold thy peace.
He that hath suffer'd this disordered spring
Hath now himself met with the fall of leaf.
The weeds which his broad-spreading leaves did shelter,   50
That seem'd in eating him to hold him up,
Are pluck'd up root and all by Bolingbroke—

---

26. **My wretchedness…pins:** Expressed in the form of a wager that gives liberal odds. 27. **state:** matters of state; politics. 28. **Against a change:** on the eve of any change in the political situation. —**forerun with:** foreshadowed by [T.P.]. 29. **apricocks:** apricots. 34. **sprays:** twigs of the shrubs [T.P.]. 38. **noisome:** noxious. —**without profit:** doing no good to anybody. 40. **in the compass of a pale:** within the limits of an enclosure—a walled garden. 42. **Showing, as in a model, our firm estate:** showing our well-established organization, as a model or pattern for the government of a kingdom. 46. **knots:** flower beds laid out in elaborate patterns. 48. **suffer'd:** permitted. 49. **the fall of leaf:** autumn. 51. **in eating him:** while they really were devouring him.

---

† *Kings* was filmed live, and this results in the incoherence of having the Gardener remove his shoulder armor as he speaks his first speech; the actor had been one of Bolingbroke's soldiers in the preceding scene. All three versions resist the temptation to make the gardeners comic rustics, as is sometimes done on stage, although *Bard'* s second gardener does a bit of mugging.

	I mean the Earl of Wiltshire, Bushy, Green.	
MAN	What, are they dead?	

GARDENER   They are; and Bolingbroke
Hath seiz'd the wasteful King. O, what pity is it   55
That he had not so trimm'd and dress'd his land
As we this garden! We at time of year
Do wound the bark, the skin of our fruit trees,
Lest, being over-proud in sap and blood,
With too much riches it confound itself.   60
Had he done so to great and growing men,
They might have liv'd to bear, and he to taste
Their fruits of duty. Superfluous branches
We lop away, that bearing boughs may live.
Had he done so, himself had borne the crown,   65
Which waste of idle hours hath quite thrown down.

MAN   What, think you the King shall be depos'd?

GARDENER   Depress'd he is already, and depos'd
'Tis doubt he will be. Letters came last night
To a dear friend of the good Duke of York's   70
That tell black tidings.

QUEEN   O, I am press'd to death through want of speaking![*Comes forward.*]
Thou old Adam's likeness, set to dress this garden,
How dares thy harsh rude tongue sound this unpleasing news?
What Eve, what serpent, hath suggested thee   75
To make a second fall of cursed man?
Why dost thou say King Richard is depos'd?
Dar'st thou, thou little better thing than earth,
Divine his downfall? Say, where, when, and how
Cam'st thou by this ill tidings? Speak, thou wretch!   80

GARDENER   Pardon me, madam. Little joy have I
To breathe this news; yet what I say is true.
King Richard, he is in the mighty hold
Of Bolingbroke. Their fortunes both are weigh'd.
In your lord's scale is nothing but himself,   85

---

56. **trimm'd and dress'd:** Synonymous: kept in orderly condition. 57. **at time of year:** at the proper time of year. 59–60. **Lest...confound itself:** lest the tree destroy itself. —**over-proud:** too luxuriant. 64. **bearing boughs:** branches that bear fruit [T.P.]. 68–69. **Depress'd:** put down; humbled. —**doubt:** fear. 72. **press'd...speaking!:** Pressing to death by laying heavy weights upon the body was the regular English penalty for "standing mute," i.e., refusing to plead guilty or not guilty. 73. **Adam's likeness:** "Adam was a gardener." 75–76. **suggested:** tempted. —**a second fall:** since the deposition of the King is as great a calamity as the fall of man. 79. **Divine:** prophesy. 82. **breathe:** utter, tell. 84. **weigh'd:** balanced against each other. 85. **scale:** pan of the balance.

And some few vanities that make him light;
But in the balance of great Bolingbroke,
Besides himself, are all the English peers,
And with that odds he weighs King Richard down.
Post you to London, and you will find it so.   90
I speak no more than every one doth know.

QUEEN   Nimble mischance, that art so light of foot,
Doth not thy embassage belong to me,
And am I last that knows it? O, thou thinkest
To serve me last, that I may longest keep   95
Thy sorrow in my breast. Come, ladies, go
To meet at London London's king in woe.
What, was I born to this, that my sad look
Should grace the triumph of great Bolingbroke?
Gard'ner, for telling me these news of woe,   100
Pray God the plants thou graft'st may never grow.
                                              Exit [with Ladies].

GARDENER   Poor Queen, so that thy state might be no worse,
I would my skill were subject to thy curse!
Here did she fall a tear; here in this place
I'll set a bank of rue, sour herb of grace.   105
Rue, even for ruth, here shortly shall be seen,
In the remembrance of a weeping queen.   *Exeunt.*

---

87. **vanities:** follies. 89. **odds:** advantage [T.P.]. 90. **Post:** travel posthaste. 93. **Doth not thy embassage belong to me?** Doth not your mission (the report you bring) pertain to me before all other persons? Why then have you brought it to everybody else first? 96. **Thy sorrow:** the sorrow that you report. 99. **Should grace the triumph:** should adorn the triumphal procession. 100. **these news:** *News* was originally plural—"new things." 102. **so:** provided that; on condition that. **—state:** condition, lot. 104. **fall:** let fall. 105. **sour:** bitter. **—herb of grace:** Rue was called "herb of grace" because to rue means to "repent" and repentance comes by the grace of God. 106. **for ruth:** as a symbol or emblem for pity.

ACT IV

Scene I. [*Westminster Hall.*]

Enter, as to the Parliament, Bolingbroke, Aumerle, Northumberland, Percy, Fitzwater, Surrey, [and another Lord, the Bishop of] Carlisle, Abbot of Westminster, Herald; Officers and Bagot.

BOLINGBROKE   Call forth Bagot.   [*Officers bring him forward.*]
Now, Bagot, freely speak thy mind,
What thou dost know of noble Gloucester's death;
Who wrought it with the King, and who perform'd
The bloody office of his timeless end.   5

BAGOT   Then set before my face the Lord Aumerle.†

BOLINGBROKE   Cousin, stand forth, and look upon that man.

BAGOT   My Lord Aumerle, I know your daring tongue
Scorns to unsay what once it hath deliver'd.
In that dead time when Gloucester's death was plotted,   10
I heard you say, "Is not my arm of length,
That reacheth from the restful English court
As far as Calais to mine uncle's head?"
Amongst much other talk that very time
I heard you say that you had rather refuse   15
The offer of an hundred thousand crowns
Than Bolingbroke's return to England;
Adding withal, how blest this land would be
In this your cousin's death.

AUMERLE   Princes and noble lords,
What answer shall I make to this base man?   20
Shall I so much dishonor my fair stars
On equal terms to give him chastisement?
Either I must, or have mine honor soil'd

ACT IV. SCENE I.
4–5. **Who wrought it with the King:** who worked it—brought it about—by influencing the King. **—who...office:** who actually performed the murderous service. **—timeless:** untimely. 9. **deliver'd:** uttered; reported. 10. **dead:** dark and dismal—not *deadly*. 11. **of length:** long. 12. **restful:** peaceful. 17. **Than Bolingbroke's return:** than for Bolingbroke to return. 18. **withal:** besides. 19. **this your cousin's:** Bolingbroke's. 20. **base:** i.e., in rank. 21. **my fair stars:** my high rank—as determined by the stars that ruled my birth. 22. **On equal terms:** as if he were my equal [T.P.]. **—to:** as to.

---

†   Only *Bard* includes the first hundred lines of accusations and challenges, pointed especially at Aumerle; this results in a large, untidy pile of gloves next to Bolingbroke's chair. Exton is given Fitzwater's lines in the text.

	With the attainder of his slanderous lips.	
	There is my gage, the manual seal of death	25
	That marks thee out for hell. I say thou liest,	
	And will maintain what thou hast said is false	
	In thy heart-blood, though being all too base	
	To stain the temper of my knightly sword.	

BOLINGBROKE Bagot, forbear; thou shalt not take it up.   30

AUMERLE Excepting one, I would he were the best
In all this presence that hath mov'd me so.

FITZWATER If that thy valor stand on sympathy,
There is my gage, Aumerle, in gage to thine.
By that fair sun which shows me where thou stand'st,   35
I heard thee say, and vauntingly thou spak'st it,
That thou wert cause of noble Gloucester's death.
If thou deniest it twenty times, thou liest,
And I will turn thy falsehood to thy heart,
Where it was forged, with my rapier's point.   40

AUMERLE Thou dar'st not, coward, live to see that day.

FITZWATER Now, by my soul, I would it were this hour.

AUMERLE Fitzwater, thou art damn'd to hell for this.

PERCY Aumerle, thou liest. His honor is as true
In this appeal as thou art all unjust;   45
And that thou art so, there I throw my gage
To prove it on thee to the extremest point
Of mortal breathing. Seize it if thou dar'st.

AUMERLE And if I do not, may my hands rot off
And never brandish more revengeful steel   50
Over the glittering helmet of my foe!

ANOTHER LORD I task thee to the like, forsworn Aumerle;
And spur thee on with full as many lies
As may be holloa'd in thy treacherous ear
From sun to sun. There is my honor's pawn.   55

---

24. **attainder:** stigma—with an allusion to the degradation and forfeiture that legally followed conviction of treason or felony. 25. **my gage:** Aumerle throws down his glove. 28–29. **being all too base... sword:** Aumerle repeats his contempt for Bagot's rank. —**the temper:** the well-tempered steel. 31. **one:** i.e., Bolingbroke. —**the best:** i.e., the highest in rank. 33. **If that...sympathy:** if your valor insist in equality of rank in your opponent. 34.**my gage:** as a pledge of defiance. 36. **vauntingly:** boastfully [T.P.]. 40. **forged:** made, referring to the falsehood. —**rapier's:** The rapier was a gentleman's weapon in Shakespeare's time, though not in that of King Richard. 45. **appeal:** accusation. —**all unjust:** altogether false. 47–48. **to...breathing:** in a combat to the death. 52. **I task thee to the like:** I challenge thee to the like—i.e., to mortal combat. 53. **lies:** assertions that you are a liar. 55. **From sun to sun:** from one sunrise to another. —**pawn:** pledge.

	Engage it to the trial, if thou dar'st.	
AUMERLE	Who sets me else? By heaven, I'll throw at all!	
	I have a thousand spirits in one breast	
	To answer twenty thousand such as you.	

SURREY   My Lord Fitzwater, I do remember well   60
           The very time Aumerle and you did talk.

FITZWATER 'Tis very true. You were in presence then,
           And you can witness with me this is true.

SURREY   As false, by heaven, as heaven itself is true!

FITZWATER Surrey, thou liest.

SURREY   Dishonorable boy!   65
           That lie shall lie so heavy on my sword
           That it shall render vengeance and revenge
           Till thou the lie-giver and that lie do lie
           In earth as quiet as thy father's skull.
           In proof whereof there is my honor's pawn.   70
           Engage it to the trial if thou dar'st.

FITZWATER How fondly dost thou spur a forward horse!
           If I dare eat, or drink, or breathe, or live,
           I dare meet Surrey in a wilderness,
           And spit upon him whilst I say he lies,   75
           And lies, and lies. There is my bond of faith
           To tie thee to my strong correction.
           As I intend to thrive in this new world,
           Aumerle is guilty of my true appeal.
           Besides, I heard the banish'd Norfolk say   80
           That thou, Aumerle, didst send two of thy men
           To execute the noble Duke at Calais.

AUMERLE   Some honest Christian trust me with a gage
           That Norfolk lies. Here do I throw down this,
           If he may be repeal'd to try his honor.   85

BOLINGBROKE These differences shall all rest under gage
           Till Norfolk be repeal'd. Repeal'd he shall be
           And, though mine enemy, restor'd again
           To all his lands and signories. When he's return'd,
           Against Aumerle we will enforce his trial.   90

---

57. **Who sets me else?** Who else challenges me?—literally, makes a wager against me? 62. **in presence:** in the King's presence chamber. 70. **pawn:** pledge. He throws down his glove. 72. **fondly:** foolishly. 74. **in a wilderness:** even in a wilderness, where no help can be had. 76. **my bond of faith:** my gage. 78. **in this new world:** i.e., under King Henry, who will restore the kingdom to order. 79. **appeal:** accusation. 89. **signories:** estates [T.P.]. 90. **trial:** i.e., by wager of battle, to which Aumerle has just challenged him.

CARLISLE   That honorable day shall ne'er be seen.
              Many a time hath banish'd Norfolk fought
              For Jesu Christ in glorious Christian field,
              Streaming the ensign of the Christian cross
              Against black pagans, Turks, and Saracens;   95
              And, toil'd with works of war, retir'd himself
              To Italy; and there, at Venice, gave
              His body to that pleasant country's earth
              And his pure soul unto his captain, Christ,
              Under whose colors he had fought so long.   100

BOLINGBROKE   Why, Bishop, is Norfolk dead?

CARLISLE   As surely as I live, my lord.

BOLINGBROKE   Sweet peace conduct his sweet soul to the bosom
              Of good old Abraham! Lords appellants,
              Your differences shall all rest under gage   105
              Till we assign you to your days of trial.

                     Enter York [attended].

YORK   Great Duke of Lancaster, I come to thee†
              From plume-pluck'd Richard, who with willing soul
              Adopts thee heir and his high sceptre yields
              To the possession of thy royal hand.   110
              Ascend his throne, descending now from him,
              And long live Henry, fourth of that name!

BOLINGBROKE   In God's name I'll ascend the regal throne.

CARLISLE   Marry, God forbid!
              Worst in this royal presence may I speak,   115
              Yet best beseeming me to speak the truth.
              Would God that any in this noble presence
              Were enough noble to be upright judge
              Of noble Richard! then true noblesse would

93–94. **Christian field:** i.e., in defense of Christianity. —**Streaming:** flying. 96. **toil'd:** worn out, exhausted. 111. **descending now from him:** which now falls to you as his heir. 114. **Marry:** Literally an oath by the Virgin Mary, but commonly used as a mere interjection. 115–16. **Worst:** with least authority and effectiveness. —**may:** can. —**best beseeming me:** i.e., because of my sacred office. 119. **noblesse:** nobility.

---

†   Both *Kings* and *BBC* begin with York's entrance and set the action in a throne room; in both
       Bolingbroke will sit on the throne—in *Kings* quite defiantly immediately after Carlisle's speech;
       in *BBC* rather unobtrusively while Northumberland gives Richard the list of crimes to which he
       is to confess. *Bard's* setting seems to be the parliament mentioned in the opening stage direction.
       Bolingbroke sits in an arm chair with Northumberland standing to his left, and most of the nobles
       seated on benches.

Learn him forbearance from so foul a wrong.   120
What subject can give sentence on his king?
And who sits here that is not Richard's subject?
Thieves are not judg'd but they are by to hear,
Although apparent guilt be seen in them;
And shall the figure of God's majesty,   125
His captain, steward, deputy elect,
Anointed, crowned, planted many years,
Be judg'd by subject and inferior breath,
And he himself not present? O, forfend it God
That, in a Christian climate, souls refin'd   130
Should show so heinous, black, obscene a deed!
I speak to subjects, and a subject speaks,
Stirr'd up by God, thus boldly for his king.
My Lord of Hereford here, whom you call king,
Is a foul traitor to proud Hereford's king;   135
And if you crown him, let me prophesy,
The blood of English shall manure the ground
And future ages groan for this foul act;
Peace shall go sleep with Turks and infidels,
And in this seat of peace tumultuous wars   140
Shall kin with kin and kind with kind confound;
Disorder, horror, fear, and mutiny
Shall here inhabit, and this land be call'd
The field of Golgotha and dead men's skulls.
O, if you raise this house against this house,   145
It will the woefullest division prove
That ever fell upon this cursed earth.
Prevent it, resist it, let it not be so,
Lest child, child's children cry against you woe.

NORTHUMBERLAND Well have you argued, sir; and for your pains   150
Of capital treason we arrest you here.
My Lord of Westminster, be it your charge
To keep him safely till his day of trial.
May it please you, lords, to grant the commons' suit.

---

120. **Learn:** teach. 123. **Thieves:** Emphatic: "even robbers." —**judg'd:** condemned. —**but they are by:** unless they are present. 124. **apparent:** manifest. 126. **elect:** chosen [T.P.]. 129. **forfend:** forbid. 130. **climate:** clime, region. —**refin'd:** purified (by Christianity). 131. **obscene:** foul. 139. **infidels:** unbelievers—i.e., heathen and Mohammedans. 141. **Shall kin with kin...confound:** shall destroy kinsmen and fellow countrymen by the hands of each other. 144. **Golgotha:** Calvary. Shakespeare adopts the explanation usual in his time that Golgotha, "a place of a skull," was so called from the many skulls of executed persons that lay about. 146. **the woefullest division:** Carlisle foretells the Wars of the Roses. 148. **Prevent:** forestall. 151. **Of:** on a charge of.

BOLINGBROKE Fetch hither Richard, that in common view   155
            He may surrender. So we shall proceed
            Without suspicion.

YORK   I will be his conduct.   *Exit.*

BOLINGBROKE Lords, you that here are under our arrest,
            Procure your sureties for your days of answer.
            Little are we beholding to your love,   160
            And little look'd for at your helping hands.

            Enter Richard and York, [with Officers bearing the crown, &c.].

RICHARD   Alack, why am I sent for to a king
            Before I have shook off the regal thoughts
            Wherewith I reign'd? I hardly yet have learn'd
            To insinuate, flatter, bow, and bend my limbs.   165
            Give sorrow leave awhile to tutor me
            To this submission. Yet I well remember
            The favors of these men. Were they not mine?
            Did they not sometime cry "All hail!" to me?
            So Judas did to Christ; but he, in twelve,   170
            Found truth in all but one; I, in twelve thousand none.
            God save the King! Will no man say amen?
            Am I both priest and clerk? Well then, amen!
            God save the King! although I be not he;
            And yet amen, if heaven do think him me.   175
            To do what service am I sent for hither?

YORK   To do that office of thine own good will
            Which tired majesty did make thee offer—
            The resignation of thy state and crown
            To Henry Bolingbroke.†   180

155–318. This famous passage—the so-called Deposition Scene—is omitted in the first three Quartos, appearing for the first time in the Quarto of 1608. However, it certainly formed a part of the play from the beginning. See Introduction. 156. **surrender:** i.e., give up the crown; abdicate. 157. **conduct:** escort. 159. **your sureties:** your guarantees of appearance at your trials by combat [T.P.]. 160. **beholding:** beholden, indebted. 168. **favors:** features. 173. **clerk:** the respondent to the priest's prayers [T.P.]. 177. **office:** service. 179. **state:** royal rank; kingship.

---

† *Bard*'s Richard surrenders the crown and the scepter, but the throne, an equally potent symbol, is nowhere to be seen. In Farrell's 2001 version, Richard mischievously drops the cap that this film substitutes for the crown just out of Bolingbroke's reach.

Richard (David Williams), right, surrenders the crown to Bolingbroke (Tom Fleming). (*Kings*, 1960.)

RICHARD   Give me the crown. Here, cousin, seize the crown.
                 Here, cousin,
                 On this side my hand, and on that side yours.
                 Now is this golden crown like a deep well
                 That owes two buckets, filling one another,   185
                 The emptier ever dancing in the air,
                 The other down, unseen, and full of water.
                 That bucket down and full of tears am I,
                 Drinking my griefs whilst you mount up on high.

BOLINGBROKE I thought you had been willing to resign.   190

RICHARD   My crown I am, but still my griefs are mine.
                 You may my glories and my state depose,
                 But not my griefs. Still am I king of those.

BOLINGBROKE Part of your cares you give me with your crown.

RICHARD   Your cares set up do not pluck my cares down.   195
                 My care is loss of care, by old care done;
                 Your care is gain of care, by new care won.
                 The cares I give I have, though given away;
                 They tend the crown, yet still with me they stay.

185. **owes:** owns. 195–199. **Your cares:** There is an elaborate pun on the two senses of *care*—(1) trouble or sorrow; (2) the worry or anxious care incident to high office. 197. **I have:** because I sorrow for their loss. 199. **They tend the crown:** They attend (accompany) the kingship—and therefore are now yours.

In John Farrell's 2001 production, Richard (Matte Osian) puckishly drops his crown/cap just out of the reach of Bolingbroke (Barry Smith).

BOLINGBROKE Are you contented to resign the crown?   200

RICHARD   Ay, no; no, ay; for I must nothing be;
                Therefore no no, for I resign to thee.
                Now mark me how I will undo myself.
                I give this heavy weight from off my head
                And this unwieldy sceptre from my hand,   205
                The pride of kingly sway from out my heart.
                With mine own tears I wash away my balm,
                With mine own hands I give away my crown,
                With mine own tongue deny my sacred state,
                With mine own breath release all duty's rites.   210
                All pomp and majesty I do forswear;
                My manors, rents, revenues I forgo;
                My acts, decrees, and statutes I deny.
                God pardon all oaths that are broke to me!
                God keep all vows unbroke that swear to thee!   215
                Make me, that nothing have, with nothing griev'd,
                And thou with all pleas'd, that hast all achiev'd!

[Handwritten marginalia: "who is he?" and "reverse currriction?"]

201–202. **Ay...no no:** The punning on *ay* and *I* allows for many possible readings. The suggestion here is that the first "Ay, no" is Richard's initial unwillingness, but the next "no, ay" is his realization that "I [ay] must nothing be"; therefore there is "no *no*"—i.e., no possibility of refusing [T.P.]. 203. **mark me:** pay attention to me, observe me [T.P.]. 207. **my balm:** the holy oil with which I was anointed at my coronation. 209. **deny my sacred state:** renounce my rank as a king by divine right. 210. **release all duty's rites:** discharge my subjects from all the ceremonies of homage and allegiance. 213. **deny:** repeal. 214. **oaths:** i.e., of allegiance. 215. **that swear:** of those who swear fealty. 217. **achiev'd:** won.

Long mayst thou live in Richard's seat to sit,
And soon lie Richard in an earthy pit!
God save King Harry, unking'd Richard says,   220
And send him many years of sunshine days!
What more remains?

NORTHUMBERLAND   No more, but that you read
These accusations and these grievous crimes
Committed by your person and your followers
Against the state and profit of this land,   225
That, by confessing them, the souls of men
May deem that you are worthily depos'd.

RICHARD   Must I do so? and must I ravel out
My weav'd-up folly? Gentle Northumberland,
If thy offences were upon record,   230
Would it not shame thee in so fair a troop
To read a lecture of them? If thou wouldst,
There shouldst thou find one heinous article,
Containing the deposing of a king
And cracking the strong warrant of an oath,   235
Mark'd with a blot, damn'd in the book of heaven.
Nay, all of you that stand and look upon
Whilst that my wretchedness doth bait myself,
Though some of you, with Pilate, wash your hands,
Showing an outward pity, yet you Pilates   240
Have here deliver'd me to my sour cross,
And water cannot wash away your sin.

NORTHUMBERLAND My lord, dispatch. Read o'er these articles.

RICHARD   Mine eyes are full of tears; I cannot see.
And yet salt water blinds them not so much   245
But they can see a sort of traitors here.
Nay, if I turn mine eyes upon myself,
I find myself a traitor with the rest;
For I have given here my soul's consent
To undeck the pompous body of a king;   250
Made glory base, and sovereignty a slave,

225. **state and profit:** "well-regulated prosperity." 226. **by confessing them:** by your confession of them. 227. **worthily:** deservedly. 228–29. **ravel out My weav'd-up folly:** unravel the texture of my folly; recount my folly in all its details. 231. **in so fair a troop:** in so fine a company. 232–33. **If thou wouldst... find:** if you were willing to read off such a list, you would certainly find in it. —**To read a lecture of them:** to read them off as if you were preaching a sermon. —**article:** item in the list. 235. **cracking... oath:** the breaking of the strong assurance given in your oath of fealty. 236. **damn'd:** condemned. 238. **bait:** torment [T.P.]. 241. **sour:** grievous. 246. **a sort:** a pack; a gang. A contemptuous word for "troop" or "company." 250. **pompous:** magnificent; clothed with royal splendor.

Proud majesty a subject, state a peasant.

NORTHUMBERLAND My lord—

RICHARD   No lord of thine, thou haught insulting man,
               Nor no man's lord. I have no name, no title—   255
               No, not that name was given me at the font—
               But 'tis usurp'd. Alack the heavy day,
               That I have worn so many winters out
               And know not now what name to call myself!
               O that I were a mockery king of snow,   260
               Standing before the sun of Bolingbroke
               To melt myself away in water drops!
               Good king, great king, and yet not greatly good,
               An if my word be sterling yet in England,
               Let it command a mirror hither straight,   265
               That it may show me what a face I have
               Since it is bankrout of his majesty.

BOLINGBROKE Go some of you and fetch a looking glass.   [*Exit an Attendant.*]

NORTHUMBERLAND Read o'er this paper while the glass doth come.

RICHARD   Fiend, thou torments me ere I come to hell!   270

BOLINGBROKE Urge it no more, my Lord Northumberland.

NORTHUMBERLAND The commons will not then be satisfied.

RICHARD   They shall be satisfied. I'll read enough
               When I do see the very book indeed
               Where all my sins are writ, and that's myself.   275

                        Enter one with a glass.

               Give me the glass, and therein will I read.
               No deeper wrinkles yet? Hath sorrow struck
               So many blows upon this face of mine
               And made no deeper wounds? O flattering glass,
               Like to my followers in prosperity,   280
               Thou dost beguile me! Was this face the face
               That every day under his household roof
               Did keep ten thousand men? Was this the face
               That like the sun did make beholders wink?

---

252. **state:** stateliness, magnificence. 254. **haught:** haughtily. 256. **No, not that name was given me at the font:** not even that name that was given me when I was christened. Richard reasons with the logic of despair and completely "undoes [i.e., unmakes] himself" (line 203). 257. **But 'tis usurp'd:** but that it is usurped. 259. **mockery:** imitation, counterfeit [T.P.]. 264. **be sterling:** pass current. 265. **straight:** straightway, immediately. 267. **bankrout:** bankrupt. **—his:** its. 283. **keep:** maintain. 284. **wink:** shut their eyes.

	Was this the face that fac'd so many follies	285
	And was at last outfac'd by Bolingbroke?	

Was this the face that fac'd so many follies   285
And was at last outfac'd by Bolingbroke?
A brittle glory shineth in this face.
As brittle as the glory is the face,   [*Dashes the glass to the floor.*]
For there it is, crack'd in a hundred shivers.
Mark, silent king, the moral of this sport—   290
How soon my sorrow hath destroy'd my face.

BOLINGBROKE The shadow of your sorrow hath destroy'd
The shadow of your face.

RICHARD   Say that again.
The shadow of my sorrow? Ha! let's see!
'Tis very true: my grief lies all within;   295
And these external manners of laments
Are merely shadows to the unseen grief
That swells with silence in the tortured soul.
There lies the substance; and I thank thee, king,
For thy great bounty that not only giv'st   300
Me cause to wail, but teachest me the way
How to lament the cause. I'll beg one boon,
And then be gone and trouble you no more.
Shall I obtain it?

BOLINGBROKE   Name it, fair cousin.

RICHARD   Fair cousin? I am greater than a king;   305
For when I was a king, my flatterers
Were then but subjects; being now a subject,
I have a king here to my flatterer.
Being so great, I have no need to beg.

BOLINGBROKE Yet ask.   310

RICHARD   And shall I have?

BOLINGBROKE You shall.

RICHARD   Then give me leave to go.

BOLINGBROKE Whither?

RICHARD   Whither you will, so I were from your sights.   315

BOLINGBROKE Go some of you, convey him to the Tower.

RICHARD   O, good! Convey? Conveyers are you all,

285–86. **fac'd:** countenanced, authorized. —**outfac'd:** discountenanced and superseded. 287. **brittle:** fragile. 292. **The shadow of your sorrow:** the sorrow that overshadows you. 296. **manners of laments:** forms of lamentation. 300. **that:** The antecedent is *thy* (= of thee). 302. **boon:** favor [T.P.]. 308. **to:** for, as. 315. **so:** provided that; if only. 317. **Conveyers:** thieves, swindlers, a polite term for "steal."

That rise thus nimbly by a true king's fall.

[Exit Richard, with some Lords and a Guard.]

BOLINGBROKE   On Wednesday next we solemnly set down
          Our coronation. Lords, prepare yourselves.   *Exeunt.* 320

Manent [the Abbot of] Westminster, [the Bishop of] Carlisle, Aumerle.

ABBOT   A woeful pageant have we here beheld.

CARLISLE   The woe's to come. The children yet unborn
          Shall feel this day as sharp to them as thorn.

AUMERLE   You holy clergymen, is there no plot
          To rid the realm of this pernicious blot?   325

ABBOT   My lord,
          Before I freely speak my mind herein,
          You shall not only take the sacrament
          To bury mine intents, but also to effect
          Whatever I shall happen to devise.   330
          I see your brows are full of discontent,
          Your hearts of sorrow, and your eyes of tears.
          Come home with me to supper. I will lay
          A plot shall show us all a merry day.   *Exeunt.*

ACT V

Scene I. [*London. A street leading to the Tower.*]

Enter the Queen with Ladies, her Attendants.

QUEEN   This way the King will come.† This is the way
          To Julius Cæsar's ill-erected tower,
          To whose flint bosom my condemned lord
          Is doom'd a prisoner by proud Bolingbroke.

---

318. **That rise…fall:** as the victim's loss is the thief's gain. 321. **pageant:** dramatic spectacle. 322. **The woe's to come:** Another prophecy of the civil wars between the House of York and the House of Lancaster. 324. **no plot:** no possible plan that can be devised. Not here used in an evil sense. 328. **take the sacrament:** This was often done to increase the sacred obligation of an oath—especially an oath of secrecy.

ACT V. SCENE I.

2. **Julius Cæsar's:** Tradition referred the erection of the Tower of London to Julius Cæsar. —**ill-erected:** Because it has been the scene of so many crimes. 3. **flint:** hard as flint; merciless.

---

†   In both *BBC* and *Bard* this is a nighttime scene lit by flickering torches and set in a street.

Here let us rest, if this rebellious earth   5
Have any resting for her true king's queen.

Enter Richard and Guard.

But soft, but see, or rather do not see,
My fair rose wither. Yet look up, behold,
That you in pity may dissolve to dew
And wash him fresh again with true-love tears.   10
Ah, thou the model where old Troy did stand,
Thou map of honor, thou King Richard's tomb,
And not King Richard! Thou most beauteous inn,
Why should hard-favor'd grief be lodg'd in thee
When triumph is become an alehouse guest?   15

RICHARD   Join not with grief, fair woman, do not so,
To make my end too sudden. Learn, good soul,
To think our former state a happy dream;
From which awak'd, the truth of what we are
Shows us but this. I am sworn brother, sweet,   20
To grim Necessity, and he and I
Will keep a league till death. Hie thee to France
And cloister thee in some religious house.
Our holy lives must win a new world's crown,
Which our profane hours here have stricken down.   25

QUEEN   What, is my Richard both in shape and mind
Transform'd and weak'ned? Hath Bolingbroke depos'd
Thine intellect? Hath he been in thy heart?
The lion dying thrusteth forth his paw
And wounds the earth, if nothing else, with rage   30
To be o'erpow'r'd; and wilt thou pupil-like
Take thy correction, mildly kiss the rod,
And fawn on rage with base humility,
Which art a lion and the king of beasts?

RICHARD   A king of beasts indeed! If aught but beasts,   35
I had been still a happy king of men.

---

6. **resting:** resting place. 7. **soft:** wait a moment. 11–12. **thou the model...stand:** As the ruins of Troy show the outlines of that magnificent city, so you, in your misery, recall to our minds what King Richard was in his days of splendor. —**map of honor:** mere outlined figure of former glory. 13–15. **Thou most beauteous inn...guest?** Richard's beauty is emphasized, and the Queen implies that this makes him the proper abode for triumph (royal splendor) in contrast to the ignoble Bolingbroke. —**hard-favor'd:** hard-featured; ugly in person and character. 18. **state:** condition of splendor. 20–22. **but this:** only this miserable condition. —**sworn brother:** Richard and Necessity are as inextricably bound together as two friends who have sworn loyalty to one another, as if they were brothers [T.P.]. 23. **religious house:** convent. 24–25. **Our holy lives...stricken down:** By living a life of devotion we must now win a new crown, a crown that our godless lives have hitherto rejected in this world. 28. **Hath he been in thy heart?** And subdued that also? 33. **rage:** i.e., thy savage enemies. 34. **Which:** who.

Good sometime queen, prepare thee hence for France.
Think I am dead, and that even here thou takest,
As from my deathbed, thy last living leave.
In winter's tedious nights sit by the fire   40
With good old folks, and let them tell thee tales
Of woeful ages long ago betid;
And ere thou bid good-night, to quite their griefs
Tell thou the lamentable tale of me,
And send the hearers weeping to their beds.   45
For why, the senseless brands will sympathize
The heavy accent of thy moving tongue
And in compassion weep the fire out;
And some will mourn in ashes, some coal-black,
For the deposing of a rightful king.   50

Enter Northumberland [attended].

NORTHUMBERLAND My lord, the mind of Bolingbroke is chang'd.
You must to Pomfret, not unto the Tower.
And, madam, there is order ta'en for you:
With all swift speed you must away to France.

RICHARD   Northumberland, thou ladder wherewithal   55
The mounting Bolingbroke ascends my throne,
The time shall not be many hours of age
More than it is, ere foul sin gathering head
Shall break into corruption. Thou shalt think,
Though he divide the realm and give thee half,   60
It is too little, helping him to all.
And he shall think that thou, which know'st the way
To plant unrightful kings, wilt know again,
Being ne'er so little urg'd, another way,
To pluck him headlong from the usurped throne.   65
The love of wicked men converts to fear;
That fear to hate, and hate turns one or both
To worthy danger and deserved death.

---

37. **sometime:** formerly, once. **—hence:** to go hence. 42. **betid:** past [T.P.]. 43. **to quite their griefs:** to requite (repay in full) their tales of woe. 46–49. **For why...sympathize...accent:** And with good reason, for even the insensate firebrands will be moved in accord with the mournful sound. **—mourn in ashes:** To scatter dust or ashes upon one's head was an old ceremony of mourning. 52. **Pomfret:** Pomfret (Pontefract) Castle in Yorkshire. 53. **there is order ta'en:** arrangements have been made. 55. **wherewithal:** by means of which. 58. **gathering head:** like a carbuncle. 61. **helping him:** since you have helped him. 64–65. **another way, To pluck:** another method of procedure (different from "planting unrightful kings")—namely, to pull him down. 66. **converts:** changes. 67. **one or both:** i.e., of the wicked men. 68. **worthy:** well-merited.

Queen Isabel (Kadina Delejalde) pushes Northumberland (Robert F. McCafferty) to his death; at least in this version she does. (Farrell, 2001.)

NORTHUMBERLAND My guilt be on my head, and there an end!
Take leave and part, for you must part forthwith.   70

RICHARD   Doubly divorc'd! Bad men, you violate
A twofold marriage—'twixt my crown and me,
And then betwixt me and my married wife.
Let me unkiss the oath 'twixt thee and me;
And yet not so, for with a kiss 'twas made.   75
Part us, Northumberland—I towards the North,
Where shivering cold and sickness pines the clime;
My wife to France, from whence, set forth in pomp,
She came adorned hither like sweet May,
Sent back like Hallowmas or short'st of day.   80

QUEEN   And must we be divided? Must we part?

RICHARD   Ay, hand from hand, my love, and heart from heart.

QUEEN   Banish us both, and send the King with me.

NORTHUMBERLAND That were some love, but little policy.

QUEEN   Then whither he goes, thither let me go.   85

RICHARD   So two, together weeping, make one woe.
Weep thou for me in France, I for thee here.

70. **part:** The first *part* means "part with each other"; the second "depart." 77. **pines the clime:** lays waste the region. 78. **pomp:** splendor, 80. **Hallowmas:** All Hallows; All Saints' Day—the first of November.

Better far off than near be ne'er the near.
Go, count thy way with sighs; I mine with groans.

QUEEN   So longest way shall have the longest moans.   90

RICHARD   Twice for one step I'll groan, the way being short,
And piece the way out with a heavy heart.
Come, come, in wooing sorrow let's be brief,
Since, wedding it, there is such length in grief.
One kiss shall stop our mouths, and dumbly part.†   95
Thus give I mine, and thus take I thy heart.

QUEEN   Give me mine own again. 'Twere no good part
To take on me to keep and kill thy heart.
So, now I have mine own again, be gone,
That I may strive to kill it with a groan.   100

RICHARD   We make woe wanton with this fond delay.
Once more adieu! The rest let sorrow say.   *Exeunt.*

Scene II. [*London. The Duke of York's Palace.*]

Enter Duke of York and the Duchess.‡

DUCHESS   My lord, you told me you would tell the rest,
When weeping made you break the story off
Of our two cousins' coming into London.

YORK   Where did I leave?

DUCHESS   At that sad stop, my lord,

---

88. **near be ne'er the near:** be near, and yet never the nearer for all that. 95. **dumbly part:** and shall make us part in silence—without bidding adieu. 97–98. **'Twere…thy heart:** It would be no good act on my part to keep your heart with me, and, instead of guarding it, to kill it, as my grief would be sure to do. 99. **now:** now that. 101. **We make woe wanton with this fond delay:** We are merely indulging our woe by playing with it in fanciful talk which is of no avail. 102. **The rest let sorrow say:** "Let grief, not words, express the rest."

ACT V. SCENE II.
3. **cousins':** Richard and Bolingbroke.

---

†   In *Kings*, Richard is led by Northumberland up a short flight of stairs and placed behind a barred
      door. Richard and his queen do not kiss in this version—the relevant lines are cut—although he
      does kiss her hand as she reaches through the bars to say goodbye.

‡   *Kings* plays only York's opening speech on the reception of Richard and Bolingbroke on their return
      to London; the balance of this scene and all of the next are cut. Both *BBC* and *Bard* play the entire
      scene. In *BBC* Charles Gray as York and Wendy Hiller as the Duchess interact very persuasively as
      an old domestic couple well attuned to each other; she hands him a handkerchief when he needs
      one. There is a fair amount of comedy is his blustering and her panic over Aumerle's conspiracy. In
      Bard, there is no such chemistry between the actors, and Aumerle is left looking like the proverbial
      deer in the headlights for most of the scene.

Where rude misgoverned hands from windows' tops   5
Threw dust and rubbish on King Richard's head.

YORK   Then, as I said, the Duke, great Bolingbroke,
Mounted upon a hot and fiery steed
Which his aspiring rider seem'd to know,
With slow but stately pace kept on his course,   10
Whilst all tongues cried "God save thee, Bolingbroke!"
You would have thought the very windows spake,
So many greedy looks of young and old
Through casements darted their desiring eyes
Upon his visage; and that all the walls   15
With painted imagery had said at once
"Jesu preserve thee! Welcome, Bolingbroke!"
Whilst he, from the one side to the other turning,
Bareheaded, lower than his proud steed's neck,
Bespake them thus, "I thank you, countrymen."   20
And thus still doing, thus he pass'd along.

DUCHESS   Alack, poor Richard! Where rode he the whilst?

YORK   As in a theatre the eyes of men,
After a well-grac'd actor leaves the stage,
Are idly bent on him that enters next,   25
Thinking his prattle to be tedious,
Even so, or with much more contempt, men's eyes
Did scowl on gentle Richard. No man cried "God save him!"
No joyful tongue gave him his welcome home,
But dust was thrown upon his sacred head;   30
Which with such gentle sorrow he shook off,
His face still combating with tears and smiles
(The badges of his grief and patience),
That, had not God for some strong purpose steel'd
The hearts of men, they must perforce have melted   35
And barbarism itself have pitied him.
But heaven hath a hand in these events,
To whose high will we bound our calm contents.
To Bolingbroke are we sworn subjects now,

---

5. **from windows' tops:** from high windows. 14. **casements:** hinged windows. 16. **painted imagery:** Human figures, labeled with words or phrases which they were supposed to be speaking, were common in the hangings (tapestry or painted cloth) that lined chamber walls. 19. **lower:** bending lower. 20. **Bespake:** addressed. 21. **still:** constantly. 24. **well-grac'd:** Since *grace* may signify "pleasing quality" as well as "favor," this phrase may combine the two meanings: "an actor who is highly esteemed (a favorite with the audience) for his excellence." 25. **idly:** heedlessly; with indifference. 33. **badges:** tokens, markers [T.P.]. 36. **barbarism itself:** even barbarians. 38. **To whose high will...contents:** and we must rest contented within whatever limits heaven's will may confine of our wishes.

Whose state and honor I for aye allow.   40

Enter Aumerle.

DUCHESS   Here comes my son Aumerle.

YORK   Aumerle that was;
But that is lost for being Richard's friend,
And, madam, you must call him Rutland now.
I am in parliament pledge for his truth
And lasting fealty to the new-made king.   45

DUCHESS   Welcome, my son. Who are the violets now
That strew the green lap of the new-come spring?

AUMERLE   Madam, I know not, nor I greatly care not.
God knows I had as lief be none as one.

YORK   Well, bear you well in this new spring of time,   50
Lest you be cropp'd before you come to prime.
What news from Oxford? Do these justs and triumphs hold?

AUMERLE   For aught I know, my lord, they do.

YORK   You will be there, I know.

AUMERLE   If God prevent not, I purpose so.   55

YORK   What seal is that that hangs without thy bosom?
Yea, look'st thou pale? Let me see the writing.

AUMERLE   My lord, 'tis nothing.

YORK   No matter then who see it.
I will be satisfied; let me see the writing.

AUMERLE   I do beseech your Grace to pardon me.   60
It is a matter of small consequence
Which for some reasons I would not have seen.

YORK   Which for some reasons, sir, I mean to see.
I fear, I fear—

DUCHESS   What should you fear?
'Tis nothing but some bond that he is ent'red into   65

---

40. **state and honor:** honorable condition of royal rank. —**for aye:** forever [T.P.]. —**allow:** accept and approve. 41–43. **Aumerle…Rutland:** He has been stripped of his title Duke of Aumerle, but retains the title of Earl of Rutland [T.P.]. 44–45. **truth:** loyalty. —**fealty:** fidelity. 46. **the violets:** i.e., the newly-created nobles. 49. **none:** not one of them. 50. **bear you:** conduct yourself [T.P.]. 51. **prime:** full bloom. 52. **Do these justs and triumphs hold?** Are these plans for tournaments and pageants finally settled? 56. **seal:** The seal of a document was affixed to a label, a strip of parchment that hung beneath its lower border. 65. **bond:** i.e., for payment on a certain day.

	For gay apparel 'gainst the triumph day.	
YORK	Bound to himself? What doth he with a bond That he is bound to? Wife, thou art a fool. Boy, let me see the writing.	
AUMERLE	I do beseech you pardon me. I may not show it.	70
YORK	I will be satisfied. Let me see it, I say.	

He plucks it out of his bosom and reads it.

	Treason, foul treason! Villain! traitor! slave!	
DUCHESS	What is the matter, my lord?	
YORK	Ho! who is within there?	

[Enter a Servant.]

	Saddle my horse. God for his mercy, what treachery is here!	75
DUCHESS	Why, what is it, my lord?	
YORK	Give me my boots, I say. Saddle my horse. *[Exit Servant.]* Now, by mine honour, by my life, by my troth, I will appeach the villain.	
DUCHESS	What is the matter?	
YORK	Peace, foolish woman.	80
DUCHESS	I will not peace. What is the matter, Aumerle?	
AUMERLE	Good mother, be content. It is no more Than my poor life must answer.	
DUCHESS	Thy life answer?	
YORK	Bring me my boots! I will unto the King.	

His Man enters with his boots.

DUCHESS	Strike him, Aumerle. Poor boy, thou art amaz'd.— Hence, villain! Never more come in my sight.	85
YORK	Give me my boots, I say! *[Servant does so and exit.]*	
DUCHESS	Why, York, what wilt thou do? Wilt thou not hide the trespass of thine own?	

---

66. **'gainst:** in preparation for. **—the triumph day:** the festal day. 67–68. **What…doth he, etc.:** Such a bond would of course be in the possession of the creditor, not the debtor. 75. **God for his mercy:** God have mercy upon us! 79. **appeach:** inform against. 82. **content:** calm. 83. **answer:** answer for. 85. **him:** i.e., the servant. **—amaz'd:** in a maze; dumbfounded. 86. **Hence, villain!** Addressed to the servant.

	Have we more sons? Or are we like to have?	90

Have we more sons? Or are we like to have?　90
Is not my teeming date drunk up with time?
And wilt thou pluck my fair son from mine age
And rob me of a happy mother's name?
Is he not like thee? Is he not thine own?

YORK　Thou fond mad woman,　95
Wilt thou conceal this dark conspiracy?
A dozen of them here have ta'en the sacrament,
And interchangeably set down their hands,
To kill the King at Oxford.

DUCHESS　　　　　　　　He shall be none;
We'll keep him here. Then what is that to him?　100

YORK　Away, fond woman! Were he twenty times
My son, I would appeach him.

DUCHESS　　　　　　　　Hadst thou groan'd for him
As I have done, thou wouldst be more pitiful.
But now I know thy mind. Thou dost suspect
That I have been disloyal to thy bed　105
And that he is a bastard, not thy son.
Sweet York, sweet husband, be not of that mind!
He is as like thee as a man may be,
Not like to me, or any of my kin,
And yet I love him.

YORK　　　　　　　Make way, unruly woman!　*Exit.* 110

DUCHESS　After, Aumerle! Mount thee upon his horse,
Spur post and get before him to the King,
And beg thy pardon ere he do accuse thee.
I'll not be long behind. Though I be old,
I doubt not but to ride as fast as York;　115
And never will I rise up from the ground
Till Bolingbroke have pardon'd thee. Away, be gone!　*Exeunt.*

Scene III. [*Windsor Castle.*]

Enter King [Henry], Percy, and other Lords.

KING HENRY　Can no man tell me of my unthrifty son?

---

91. **my teeming date:** my time for bearing children. —**drunk up:** exhausted. 95. **fond:** foolish. 98. **interchangeably set down their hands:** reciprocally signed their names [T.P.]. 99. **He shall be none:** He shall not be one of them. 111. **his horse:** one of his horses. 112. **post:** posthaste.
ACT V. SCENE III.
1. **unthrifty:** A mild word for "dissolute."

'Tis full three months since I did see him last.
If any plague hang over us, 'tis he.
I would to God, my lords, he might be found.
Inquire at London, 'mongst the taverns there,   5
For there, they say, he daily doth frequent,
With unrestrained loose companions,
Even such, they say, as stand in narrow lanes
And beat our watch and rob our passengers,
Which he, young wanton and effeminate boy,   10
Takes on the point of honor to support
So dissolute a crew.

PERCY   My lord, some two days since I saw the Prince
And told him of those triumphs held at Oxford.

KING HENRY   And what said the gallant?   15

PERCY   His answer was, he would unto the stews,
And from the common'st creature pluck a glove
And wear it as a favor, and with that
He would unhorse the lustiest challenger.

KING HENRY   As dissolute as desperate! Yet through both   20
I see some sparks of better hope, which elder years
May happily bring forth. But who comes here?

Enter Aumerle, amazed.

AUMERLE   Where is the King?†

KING HENRY   What means our cousin, that he stares and looks
So wildly?   25

AUMERLE   God save your Grace! I do beseech your Majesty

---

6. **frequent:** resort. 7. **unrestrained loose companions:** lawless fellows. *Companion* is often used in a contemptuous sense. 9. **watch:** watchmen; guards [T.P.]. —**passengers:** passers-by. 10. **Which:** whom. —**wanton:** A noun: "prodigal." 14. **held:** appointed to be held. 16. **stews:** brothels. 17. **commonest creature:** most disreputable prostitute [T.P.]. 18. **a favor:** a token of a lady's favor. 19. **lustiest:** most stalwart. 22. **happily:** perhaps [T.P.]. 27. **conference:** conversation [T.P.].

---

†   *BBC* cuts the opening discussion of Bolingbroke's "unthrifty son," to begin with Aumerle's entrance. The by-play between Gray and Hiller is intensified: she pushes him away, tries to screen him from Bolingbroke's sight, and comically overwhelms his puffing and blowing with her volubility. Jon Finch as Bolingbroke varies from embarrassment, amusement, and impatience during the pleas, and after the others have exited, screams, hands to head, in exasperation. *Bard* includes the opening lines between Bolingbroke and Harry Percy, and even has the latter speak to the camera a couple of lines from *Henry IV, Part 1* on his rivalry with Prince Hal. (It is hard to see why these are included beyond the actor's simply wanting to say them.) Nan Martin as the Duchess is effective and a touch comic in her strident insistence that Bolingbroke concern himself not with her kneeling, but with the business of pardoning Aumerle. Paul Shenar as Bolingbroke is, like Jon Finch, successful in portraying the new king's various emotions.

                To have some conference with your Grace alone.

King Henry   Withdraw yourselves and leave us here alone.
                                      [Exeunt Percy and Lords.]
                What is the matter with our cousin now?

Aumerle   For ever may my knees grow to the earth,   *[Kneels.]* 30
                My tongue cleave to the roof within my mouth,
                Unless a pardon ere I rise or speak.

King Henry   Intended, or committed, was this fault?
                If on the first, how heinous e'er it be,
                To win thy after-love I pardon thee.   35

Aumerle   Then give me leave that I may turn the key,
                That no man enter till my tale be done.

King Henry   Have thy desire.

      [Aumerle locks the door.] The Duke of York knocks at the door and crieth.

York   *(within)* My liege, beware! look to thyself!
                Thou hast a traitor in thy presence there.   40

King Henry   Villain, I'll make thee safe.   *[Draws.]*

Aumerle   Stay thy revengeful hand; thou hast no cause to fear.

York   *(within)* Open the door, secure foolhardy king!
                Shall I for love speak treason to thy face?
                Open the door, or I will break it open!   45

                              Enter York.

King Henry   What is the matter, uncle? Speak.
                Recover breath; tell us how near is danger,
                That we may arm us to encounter it.

York   Peruse this writing here, and thou shalt know
                The treason that my haste forbids me show.   50

Aumerle   Remember, as thou read'st, thy promise pass'd.
                I do repent me. Read not my name there.
                My heart is not confederate with my hand.

York   It was, villain, ere thy hand did set it down.
                I tore it from the traitor's bosom, King.   55
                Fear, and not love, begets his penitence.

---

32. **Unless a pardon:** i.e., you grant a pardon [T.P.]. 34. **on the first:** of the former kind—i.e., "intended." 41. **safe:** harmless. 42. **revengeful:** avenging. 43. **secure:** heedless 50. **my haste:** which makes me breathless, so that I cannot tell you the story in full. 51. **pass'd:** already given. 53. **hand:** handwriting. 57. **Forget to pity him:** Forget any thought of showing him mercy.

Forget to pity him, lest thy pity prove
A serpent that will sting thee to the heart.

KING HENRY   O heinous, strong, and bold conspiracy!
O loyal father of a treacherous son!   60
Thou sheer, immaculate, and silver fountain,
From whence this stream through muddy passages
Hath held his current and defil'd himself!
Thy overflow of good converts to bad,
And thy abundant goodness shall excuse   65
This deadly blot in thy digressing son.

YORK   So shall my virtue be his vice's bawd,
And he shall spend mine honor with his shame,
As thriftless sons their scraping father's gold.
Mine honor lives when his dishonor dies,   70
Or my sham'd life in his dishonor lies.
Thou kill'st me in his life; giving him breath,
The traitor lives, the true man's put to death.

DUCHESS   (*within*) What ho, my liege! For God's sake let me in!

KING HENRY   What shrill-voic'd suppliant makes this eager cry?   75

DUCHESS   (*within*) A woman, and thy aunt, great King. 'Tis I.
Speak with me, pity me, open the door!
A beggar begs that never begg'd before.

KING HENRY   Our scene is alt'red from a serious thing,
And now chang'd to "The Beggar and the King."   80
My dangerous cousin, let your mother in.
I know she is come to pray for your foul sin.

YORK   If thou do pardon, whosoever pray,
More sins for this forgiveness prosper may.
This fest'red joint cut off, the rest rest sound;   85
This let alone will all the rest confound.

Enter Duchess.

---

58. **A serpent:** An allusion to the old fable of the man who warmed a half-frozen serpent by putting it in the bosom of his garment and was stung to death by the snake. 61. **sheer:** clear, pure. 62. **this stream:** With a gesture indicating Aumerle. 64. **Thy overflow of good:** your excessive goodness. — **converts:** changes (in your son). 66. **thy digressing son:** your wayward son; your son who departs from the loyalty that he should have inherited from his father. 67. **bawd:** procurer; go-between [T.P.]. 68. **he shall spend mine honor with his shame:** since his shameful treason will always disgrace my honorable loyalty. —**scraping:** frugal [T.P.]. 70. **lives:** comes to life. 71. **lies:** is involved in. 75. **cry:** outcry. 79–80. **Our scene:** the course of our drama. —**The Beggar and the King:** A punning allusion to the old song of "King Cophetua and the Beggar Maid." 85. **rest:** remain. 86. **let alone:** left untreated [T.P.]. —**confound:** destroy.

DUCHESS	O King, believe not this hard-hearted man!
	Love loving not itself, none other can.
YORK	Thou frantic woman, what dost thou make here?
	Shall thy old dugs once more a traitor rear?	90
DUCHESS	Sweet York, be patient. Hear me, gentle liege. [*Kneels.*]
KING HENRY	Rise up, good aunt.
DUCHESS	Not yet, I thee beseech.
	For ever will I walk upon my knees,
	And never see day that the happy sees,
	Till thou give joy, until thou bid me joy	95
	By pardoning Rutland, my transgressing boy.
AUMERLE	Unto my mother's prayers I bend my knee. [*Kneels.*]
YORK	Against them both my true joints bended be. [*Kneels.*]
	Ill mayst thou thrive if thou grant any grace!
DUCHESS	Pleads he in earnest? Look upon his face.	100
	His eyes do drop no tears, his prayers are in jest;
	His words come from his mouth, ours from our breast.
	He prays but faintly and would be denied;
	We pray with heart and soul and all beside:
	His weary joints would gladly rise, I know;	105
	Our knees shall kneel till to the ground they grow.
	His prayers are full of false hypocrisy;
	Ours of true zeal and deep integrity.
	Our prayers do outpray his; then let them have
	That mercy which true prayer ought to have.	110
KING HENRY	Good aunt, stand up.
DUCHESS	Nay, do not say "stand up."
	Say "pardon" first, and afterwards "stand up."
	An if I were thy nurse, thy tongue to teach,
	"Pardon" should be the first word of thy speech.
	I never long'd to hear a word till now.	115
	Say "pardon," King; let pity teach thee how.
	The word is short, but not so short as sweet;
	No word like "pardon" for kings' mouths so meet.
YORK	Speak it in French, King. Say "Pardonne moi."

---

88. **Love...can:** Since he has no love for Aumerle, his own flesh and blood, it is impossible that he should love anybody. 89. **what dost thou make?** what are you doing? 91. **patient:** calm. 93. **For ever will I walk upon my knees:** never rise from kneeling. 98. **true:** loyal. 110. **true:** sincere. 118. **meet:** fitting; appropriate [T.P.]. 119. **'Pardonne moi.':** A courteous form of refusal, like our "excuse me."

DUCHESS	Dost thou teach pardon pardon to destroy? 120
	Ah, my sour husband, my hard-hearted lord,
	That sets the word itself against the word!
	Speak "pardon" as 'tis current in our land;
	The chopping French we do not understand.
	Thine eye begins to speak, set thy tongue there; 125
	Or in thy piteous heart plant thou thine ear,
	That hearing how our plaints and prayers do pierce,
	Pity may move thee "pardon" to rehearse.
KING HENRY	Good aunt, stand up.
DUCHESS	I do not sue to stand.
	Pardon is all the suit I have in hand. 130
KING HENRY	I pardon him as God shall pardon me.
DUCHESS	O happy vantage of a kneeling knee!
	Yet am I sick for fear. Speak it again.
	Twice saying "pardon" doth not pardon twain,
	But makes one pardon strong.
KING HENRY	With all my heart 135
	I pardon him.
DUCHESS	A god on earth thou art. *[Rises.]*
KING HENRY	But for our trusty brother-in-law and the Abbot,
	With all the rest of that consorted crew,
	Destruction straight shall dog them at the heels.
	Good uncle, help to order several powers, 140
	To Oxford, or where'er these traitors are.
	They shall not live within this world, I swear,
	But I will have them, if I once know where.
	Uncle, farewell; and, cousin, adieu.
	Your mother well hath pray'd, and prove you true. 145
DUCHESS	Come, my old son. I pray God make thee new. *Exeunt.*

---

121. **sour:** bitter (in disposition). 122. **sets the word itself against the word:** makes the word pardon contradict itself. 123. **Speak 'pardon':** Addressed to the King. 124. **chopping:** changeable, shifting, ambiguous. 125. **to speak:** i.e., to express pity. —**set thy tongue there...ear:** Let your tongue speak as your eye speaks, or listen to the dictates of your compassionate heart. 128. **rehearse:** repeat [T.P.]. 129. **sue:** beg, petition [T.P.]. 131. **shall pardon me:** i.e., for all my sins at the Day of Judgment. 137–39. **for:** as for. —**brother-in-law:** the Duke of Exeter, the husband of King Henry's sister Elizabeth. —**the Abbot:** i.e., of Westminster. —**consorted:** Consort (noun or verb) often has a scornful suggestion. —**straight:** straightway. 140–41. **to order several powers, To Oxford, etc.:** to make ready a number of different troops—to be sent to Oxford or elsewhere. 146. **Old:** *Old* refers not to his age but to his character. The Duchess hopes that this may be changed for the better.

Scene IV. [*Windsor Castle.*]

Enter Sir Pierce Exton and Servant.†

EXTON   Didst thou not mark the King, what words he spake?
          "Have I no friend will rid me of this living fear?"
          Was it not so?

MAN   These were his very words.

EXTON   "Have I no friend?" quoth he. He spake it twice
          And urg'd it twice together, did he not?

MAN   He did.   5

EXTON   And speaking it, he wishtly look'd on me,
          As who should say, "I would thou wert the man
          That would divorce this terror from my heart!"
          Meaning the king at Pomfret. Come, let's go.
          I am the King's friend, and will rid his foe.   10

ACT V. SCENE IV.
1. **mark:** hear [T.P.]. 6. **wishtly:** expectantly; hopefully [T.P.]. 10. **rid:** get rid of [T.P.].

---

†   *Kings* gives us just a two-shot of a pair of actors we have not previously seen; its Exton is villainous-looking, but there is no real clue as to whether Bolingbroke has in fact commissioned him to kill Richard. *BBC* also gives us two new actors, but their location next to a pillar in a high-ceilinged vestibule, and perhaps thirty or forty feet away from Bolingbroke, who is seen passing in the back of the shot, may hint at a comparable distance of Exton from the new king's intentions. In *Bard*, Exton has been seen several times as Bolingbroke's energetic and sometimes brutal supporter, so his claim to have read the king's hint properly may well seem to have some substance.

A Christ-like Richard (David William) imprisoned in Pomfret Castle. (*Kings*, 1960.)

Scene V. [*Pomfret Castle.*]

Enter Richard, alone.

RICHARD I have been studying how I may compare
    This prison where I live unto the world;[†]
    And, for because the world is populous,
    And here is not a creature but myself,
    I cannot do it. Yet I'll hammer it out.   5
    My brain I'll prove the female to my soul,
    My soul the father; and these two beget
    A generation of still-breeding thoughts;
    And these same thoughts people this little world,
    In humours like the people of this world,   10

ACT V. SCENE V.
3. **for because:** for the reason that. 5. **hammer it out:** work it out; make it work [T.P.]. 6–10. **My brain…
this world:** My feelings (the emotions of my soul) act upon my brain, and the result is thoughts. These thoughts are still-breeding (i.e., they incessantly produce other thoughts); and thus this little world (my prison) is populated by thoughts which resemble, in their dispositions, the people of the actual world; for they are never quite happy and contented.

---

† *BBC* deliberately breaks Richard's soliloquy into sections: the camera shot is dissolved eight or nine times, to present Jacobi in different postures or in different locations or from a different camera angle. The cell is fairly spacious with a grille at one end and a cell door at the other; a large crucifix is displayed on the wall. The fight with the assassins is much extended and there is a great deal of fencing with halberds; the action is not convincing.

For no thought is contented. The better sort,
As thoughts of things divine, are intermix'd
With scruples, and do set the word itself
Against the word:
As thus, "Come, little ones," and then again,   15
"It is as hard to come as for a camel
To thread the postern of a small needle's eye."
Thoughts tending to ambition, they do plot
Unlikely wonders—how these vain weak nails
May tear a passage through the flinty ribs   20
Of this hard world, my ragged prison walls;
And, for they cannot, die in their own pride.
Thoughts tending to content flatter themselves
That they are not the first of fortune's slaves,
Nor shall not be the last; like seely beggars   25
Who, sitting in the stocks, refuge their shame,
That many have, and others must sit there.
And in this thought they find a kind of ease,
Bearing their own misfortunes on the back
Of such as have before endur'd the like.   30
Thus play I in one person many people,
And none contented. Sometimes am I king:
Then treasons make me wish myself a beggar,
And so I am. Then crushing penury
Persuades me I was better when a king;   35
Then am I king'd again; and by-and-by
Think that I am unking'd by Bolingbroke,
And straight am nothing. But whate'er I be,
Nor I, nor any man that but man is,
With nothing shall be pleas'd till he be eas'd   40
With being nothing.   *The music plays.*
                    Music do I hear?
Ha, ha! keep time. How sour sweet music is

---

12. **As:** such as. 13–14. **scruples:** doubts and difficulties. —**set the word itself Against the word:** i.e., by finding what they think are contradictions in the Bible (*God's* word) itself. 15. **"Come, little ones.":** "Jesus said, Suffer little children, and forbid them not, to come unto me: for of such is the kingdom of heaven" (*Matthew*, xix, 14). 16–17. **"It is as hard to come...eye.":** "And again I say unto you, it is easier for a camel to go through the eye of a needle, than for a rich man to enter into the kingdom of God" (*Matthew*, xix, 24). —**postern:** a small back gate. 19. **vain:** worthless [T.P.]. 21. **ragged:** rough. 22. **for they cannot:** because they cannot contrive how that may be done. —**die in their own pride:** in their prime; while still in full vigor. 25–26. **seely:** a form of silly, "simple." —**refuge their shame:** find a refuge from their disgrace. 36. **by-and-by:** in a moment; next moment. 37. **unking'd:** deposed. 40. **With nothing shall be pleas'd:** shall never be fully satisfied with anything in this life. —**With being nothing:** i.e., by ceasing to exist.

When time is broke and no proportion kept!
So is it in the music of men's lives.
And here have I the daintiness of ear   45
To check time broke in a disordered string;
But, for the concord of my state and time,
Had not an ear to hear my true time broke.
I wasted time, and now doth time waste me;
For now hath time made me his numb'ring clock: 50
My thoughts are minutes; and with sighs they jar
Their watches on unto mine eyes, the outward watch,
Whereto my finger, like a dial's point,
Is pointing still, in cleansing them from tears.
Now, sir, the sounds that tell what hour it is   55
Are clamorous groans, that strike upon my heart,
Which is the bell. So sighs and tears and groans
Show minutes, times, and hours. But my time
Runs posting on in Bolingbroke's proud joy,
While I stand fooling here, his Jack o' th' clock.   60
This music mads me. Let it sound no more;
For though it have holp madmen to their wits,
In me it seems it will make wise men mad.
Yet blessing on his heart that gives it me!
For 'tis a sign of love, and love to Richard   65
Is a strange brooch in this all-hating world.

Enter a Groom of the stable.

GROOM   Hail, royal prince!†

---

45. **daintiness:** delicacy [T.P.]. 46. **check:** rebuke, find fault with. —**a disordered string:** a stringed instrument played badly [T.P.]. 47. **for:** with reference to. —**my state and time:** my government of the realm and my life. 51–54. **My thoughts…:** Every minute of my life has its own sad thought that makes me sigh. By these sighs (which are the ticks of the clock) my thoughts communicate their wakefulness to my eyes. My eyes are "the outward watch" (i.e., the marks round the clock's dial) and to these my finger (like the minute hard) always points, for with every sigh it wipes away a tear. 58. **times:** divisions of the hours—quarters and halves. —**my time:** my life. 59. **Runs posting on…joy:** My life (of sorrow) runs on with speed in the joyful reign of Bolingbroke. 60. **Jack o' th' clock:** a grotesque human figure that stands outside the clock-case and strikes the hours on a bell. 61. **mads me:** drives me mad. 62. **holp:** helped. 63. **wise:** sane. 66. **a strange brooch:** an adornment that few men wear. *Brooches* were worn in the hat. —**this all-hating world:** this world in which everybody hates me.

---

†   *Bard* also frequently changes camera angles, though less so than *BBC*, and again there is a large crucifix on the wall. The cell is actually a room with wooden walls, and we first see Richard, wrapped in a blanket and shivering, through the barred opening in the ceiling above him. *Bard* returns to this camera angle for the visit of the Groom, who hands down a white rose to Richard, for Exton's fatal spear thrust down through the opening, and for our final view of Richard. Once the murderers appear, Richard throws off his blanket and is revealed to be naked but for a white loin cloth. After dueling with the attackers—the detail of the fight is much like *BBC*'s—Richard dies, lying on his back with his arms stretched out in the posture of the crucified Christ (see illustration, p. 97). The tableau is repeated as the final shot of the *Bard* version.

RICHARD   Thanks, noble peer.
               The cheapest of us is ten groats too dear.
               What art thou? and how comest thou hither,
               Where no man never comes but that sad dog   70
               That brings me food to make misfortune live?

GROOM   I was a poor groom of thy stable, King,
               When thou wert king; who, travelling towards York,
               With much ado, at length, have gotten leave
               To look upon my sometimes royal master's face.   75
               O, how it ern'd my heart when I beheld,
               In London streets, that coronation day,
               When Bolingbroke rode on roan Barbary,
               That horse that thou so often hast bestrid,
               That horse that I so carefully have dress'd!   80

RICHARD   Rode he on Barbary? Tell me, gentle friend,
               How went he under him?

GROOM   So proudly as if he had disdain'd the ground.

RICHARD   So proud that Bolingbroke was on his back!
               That jade hath eat bread from my royal hand;   85
               This hand hath made him proud with clapping him.
               Would he not stumble? Would he not fall down
               (Since pride must have a fall) and break the neck
               Of that proud man that did usurp his back?
               Forgiveness, horse! Why do I rail on thee,   90
               Since thou, created to be aw'd by man,
               Wast born to bear? I was not made a horse;
               And yet I bear a burthen like an ass,
               Spurr'd, gall'd and tir'd by jaucing Bolingbroke.

                         Enter Keeper, with a dish.

KEEPER   Fellow, give place. Here is no longer stay.   95

RICHARD   If thou love me, 'tis time thou wert away.

GROOM   What my tongue dares not, that my heart shall say.   *Exit.*

KEEPER   My lord, will't please you to fall to?

---

68. **The cheapest of us is ten groats too dear:** A *groat* was fourpence. A *royal* was a coin worth ten shillings (120 pence); a *noble* was worth six shillings and eightpence (80 pence). The difference between a royal and a noble, then, would be ten groats (40 pence). 70. **sad dog:** dismal fellow. 75. **sometimes royal:** sometime (i.e., formerly) royal. 76. **ern'd:** grieved. 80. **dress'd:** groomed. 85. **jade:** nag; a contemptuous term for "horse.". 86. **with clapping:** by patting. 94. **gall'd:** made sore. —**jaucing:** making the horse prance. 98. **to fall to:** to begin eating.

The dead Richard (David Birney) in the attitude of a crucifixion. (*Bard*, 1981.)

RICHARD   Taste of it first, as thou art wont to do.

KEEPER   My lord, I dare not. Sir Pierce of Exton,   100
Who lately came from the King, commands the contrary.

RICHARD   The devil take Henry of Lancaster, and thee!
Patience is stale, and I am weary of it.   [*Beats the Keeper.*]

KEEPER   Help, help, help!
Exton and Servants, the Murderers, rush in.

RICHARD   How now! What means death in this rude assault?   105
Villain, thy own hand yields thy death's instrument.
[*Snatches a weapon from a Servant and kills him.*]
Go thou and fill another room in hell.
[*Kills another.*] *Here Exton strikes him down.*
That hand shall burn in never-quenching fire
That staggers thus my person.† Exton, thy fierce hand

99. **Taste of it first:** i.e., to prove that the food is not poisoned. 105. **What means death in this rude assault?** Death is personified. "What does Death mean by assailing me so violently?" 107. **room:** place, space.

† *Kings* proceeds more simply. The camera tracks in through the bars of Richard's cell to show him seated on the straw. David William will remain seated until the sounding of the music, at which he comes forward and is framed in a rectangle of the bars. William wears a long white robe and with his shoulder length hair and light beard—he had a rather stylish goatee earlier in the play—he very much recalls the traditional image of Christ (see illustration, p. 93). The fight is a good deal less violent: Richard's back, up against the bars, screens most of it. He is turned face forward to receive Exton's death blow, with his arms spread out against the bars. Richard's last lines are gasped out very naturalistically, with blood trickling from his mouth. *Kings'* simplicity of presentation is quite effective.

| | Hath with the King's blood stain'd the King's own land. | 110 |

Mount, mount, my soul! thy seat is up on high;

Whilst my gross flesh sinks downward, here to die.   *[Dies.]*

EXTON   As full of valor as of royal blood.

Both have I spill'd. O, would the deed were good!

For now the devil, that told me I did well,   115

Says that this deed is chronicled in hell.

This dead king to the living king I'll bear.

Take hence the rest, and give them burial here.   *Exeunt.*

Scene VI. [*Windsor Castle.*]

Flourish. Enter Bolingbroke [as King], the Duke of York, with other Lords, and Attendants.

KING   Kind uncle York, the latest news we hear

Is that the rebels have consum'd with fire

Our town of Ciceter in Gloucestershire;†

But whether they be ta'en or slain we hear not.

Enter Northumberland.

Welcome, my lord. What is the news?   5

NORTHUMBERLAND First, to thy sacred state wish I all happiness.

The next news is, I have to London sent

The heads of Oxford, Salisbury, Blunt, and Kent.

The manner of their taking may appear

At large discoursed in this paper here.‡   10

KING   We thank thee, gentle Percy, for thy pains

And to thy worth will add right worthy gains.

Enter Lord Fitzwater.

FITZWATER   My lord, I have from Oxford sent to London

The heads of Brocas and Sir Bennet Seely,

ACT V. SCENE VI.
2. **consum'd:** destroyed. 3. **Ciceter:** Cirencester. 6. **state:** royalty. 10. **At large discoursed:** fully explained [T.P.].

---

† Both *BBC* and *Bard* begin with Bolingbroke on his throne, receiving the news of the failed plot against him. *Kings* has Bolingbroke seated at the table that had been used for Richard in the opening scene. Since this version had cut the discussion between Bolingbroke and Harry Percy about "my unthrifty son" (5.3.1*ff*), it is inserted here.

‡ *Kings*, unlike the other versions, was part of a series, and some preparation for the next play, *Henry IV, Part 1*, was provided. This concern seems to lie behind Northumberland's presenting a document reporting his success against Bolingbroke's enemies and Bolingbroke, rather ostentatiously, ignoring the document. They will of course be enemies in the next play.

| | Two of the dangerous consorted traitors | 15 |
| | That sought at Oxford thy dire overthrow. | |

KING
Thy pains, Fitzwater, shall not be forgot.
Right noble is thy merit, well I wot.

Enter Henry Percy and [the Bishop of] Carlisle.

PERCY
The grand conspirator, Abbot of Westminster,
With clog of conscience and sour melancholy   20
Hath yielded up his body to the grave;
But here is Carlisle living, to abide
Thy kingly doom and sentence of his pride.

KING
Carlisle, this is your doom:
Choose out some secret place, some reverend room,   25
More than thou hast, and with it joy thy life.
So, as thou liv'st in peace, die free from strife;
For though mine enemy thou hast ever been,
High sparks of honor in thee have I seen.

Enter Exton, with [Attendants bearing] a coffin.†

EXTON
Great King, within this coffin I present   30
Thy buried fear. Herein all breathless lies
The mightiest of thy greatest enemies,
Richard of Bordeaux, by me hither brought.

KING
Exton, I thank thee not; for thou hast wrought
A deed of slander, with thy fatal hand,   35
Upon my head and all this famous land.

EXTON
From your own mouth, my lord, did I this deed.

KING
They love not poison that do poison need,

---

15. **consorted:** joined together illicitly [T.P.]. 20. **clog of conscience:** the burden of a guilty conscience. 25. **secret place:** place of retirement, such as a monastery. **—some reverend room:** some place dedicated to the religious life. 26. **More than thou hast:** different from any place of residence that you already possess. **—joy:** enjoy. 29. **High:** noble. 31. **fear:** object of fear. 35. **A deed of slander:** a deed that brings disgrace.

---

† In *BBC*, we are given a shot from a position high, behind and to the right of the throne as Exton enters with the coffin. When the coffin is opened there seems to be a sheet of lead over the body, with the face or a death mask of the victim visible. The final shot is Bolingbroke, with Carlisle and Aumerle, kneeling by the coffin. In *Bard*, Exton appears unexpectedly with the coffin on the platform above and to the left of the throne. Bolingbroke climbs a flight of stairs, and follows the coffin and its bearers. In *Kings*, Exton's arrival brings Bolingbroke to a window, from which he looks down ten feet or so to the coffin in which Richard's body is displayed. The corpse on a lower and darker level has a nice symbolic implication. The aggrieved Northumberland again presents his document as Bolingbroke leaves to mourn Richard. He pushes past the frustrated Northumberland, who throws the paper on the table, picks up a knife, and stabs it into the report of his disregarded service. The paper impaled by the knife is the final shot.

Nor do I thee. Though I did wish him dead,
I hate the murtherer, love him murthered.   40
The guilt of conscience take thou for thy labor,
But neither my good word nor princely favor.
With Cain go wander thorough shades of night,
And never show thy head by day nor light.
Lords, I protest my soul is full of woe   45
That blood should sprinkle me to make me grow.
Come, mourn with me for what I do lament,
And put on sullen black incontinent.
I'll make a voyage to the Holy Land
To wash this blood off from my guilty hand.   50
March sadly after. Grace my mournings here
In weeping after this untimely bier.   *Exeunt.*

---

43. **thorough:** through. 48. **sullen:** gloomy, mournful. —**incontinent:** forthwith. 51. **Grace:** do honor
to.

HOW TO READ *THE TRAGEDY OF KING RICHARD THE SECOND* AS PERFORMANCE

Reading the play as performance ideally should mean mounting a full-fledged enactment of *Richard II* in the theater of your own imagination. Minimally it should mean keeping alive in your reading the sense that the words of the play are the speeches of various humans in a great variety of situations.

That you should do something like this is suggested by what we know of Shakespeare's own operation. He seems to have cared very little indeed whether people read his plays, although, of course, as a working playwright, actor, and theatrical producer, he had to have cared enormously whether people came to see them performed. It seems astonishing to us—for whom "Shakespeare" tends to mean long blocks of intricate if eloquent words on a page—that Shakespeare himself left just about half of his dramatic output unpublished during his lifetime. Even this might be overstating the matter, since acting companies rather than individual authors ordinarily arranged for play publication. There were, to be sure, a large number of quartos (the small, cheaply made format in which individual plays were printed) of the Shakespeare plays that were in fact printed—he was popular in this sense as well—but none of these many editions gives us evidence that Shakespeare was involved as author/editor in providing an accurate text for his readers. This is, incidentally, very much not the case with the publication of Shakespeare's narrative poems, *Venus and Adonis* and *The Rape of Lucrece*, both dedicated to the Earl of Southampton, and both printed carefully and, we think, with Shakespeare's involvement, by his neighbor from Stratford, Richard Field.

Reading *Richard II* as performance should at the least mean keeping in one's mind a sense of the sound of the words being read. One can, depending on the immediate social setting, read the words aloud; equally well, one could read them with others. If the opportunity presents itself, obviously, viewing a filmed or a live performance would be even more valuable. Fortunately, current technology provides an even easier alternative. There are good audio versions of all of Shakespeare's plays produced by companies like Arkangel or Audio Books. Once loaded into an iPod and connected to an earpiece, it becomes just about literally possible to put Shakespeare's words into one's head.

The theater of the imagination also clearly invites the visual as well as the auditory, and fortunately, this theater has no budgetary constraints. *Richard II* is no more than moderately epic at best; unlike the majority of Shakespeare's histories, it has no big battle scene. Still, it has a number of settings that ask for appropriate imaginary or theatrical realization: there is the throne room, rich and ceremonial, which begins the play, and which will be revisited with both remembrance and change for the deposition scene and the finale in which Richard's coffin is brought on stage. There is also is the pageantry of the lists at Coventry, and the spatial confrontation at Flint Castle, with Richard above and Bolingbroke below in the base court. Contrasted to this fullness and richness, there are the scenes of desolation on the Welsh coast as Richard's power disappears, and there is, of course, the bleakness of his prison. Even in the gardeners' scene, the lecture on the order of the garden in contrast to the disorder of Richard's reign may well be visually underlined by what we are shown. Achieving something like what has just been described is what traditionally has been attempted in theatrical productions of *Richard II*, and this is basically what Cedric Messina, in describing his goals for the BBC *Richard* (and for the series generally) decided on: a production that was relatively realistic, unstylized, set in generally contemporary costuming and locale. Messina thought of this kind of production as permanently available, and implicitly, permanently valuable. Peter Dews' *Age of Kings*, though somewhat constrained by the permanent set and the general limitation of resources, intended and achieved something quite similar.

The *Bard* version attempted to recapture something of the original staging of Shakespeare's time by playing on a bare stage, with rich costumes but no scenery. For a brief period at the beginning of the performance *Bard* may have captured something of the fluidity and neutrality of Shakespeare's stage, but it is hardly possible to remain as tightly limited later in the version; using a camera virtually demands kinds of views that could not have occurred in Shakespeare's Globe. Elizabethan "original practices" create so unfamiliar a location that for a modern reader or audience, the mere strangeness of the performance may well be virtually all that it communicates. There are some clips available on YouTube of the 2008 *Richard II*, performed at the rebuilt Globe with Mark Rylance in the title role. One is likely to be extremely impressed with what the Elizabethans made of the seemingly limited presence of the actor alone on the bare stage, but drawing remarkably on his own set of skills in rendering the language and displaying his own very considerable physical abilities. Rylance makes a curiously pawky Richard—he is an actor of great resource and perhaps equal eccentricity—but his ability to command a live audience while sitting on a stool on an empty stage must be something like the command that the greatest of Elizabethan actors possessed.

Backdating to Shakespeare's own time can present problems; so too can updating to other times. The Bogdanov-Pennington *Wars of the Roses* of the late 1980s staged its *Richard II* in Regency times, which evoked an impression of privileged irresponsibility that worked well enough, at least at the beginning. But once we get to the duel, the world of Beau Brummel and Lord Byron seems an odd place for what we hear of warhorses, lances, and chivalry. In general, updating runs into the problem that, however ingeniously the analogues of one time seem to fit the corresponding elements in the original, still, similar things are ultimately different things, and difference almost inevitably will assert itself. With John Farrell's 2001 film, it is difficult to see the analogy between Richard's late medieval world and the "non-society" presented here.

There are, unfortunately, a couple of special problems that might make reading *Richard II* as a performance more difficult than usual for a Shakespeare play. There is in *Richard II* very little action, until of course Richard's murder. This means that for this play the blocking—the arrangement of the characters relative to one another—is especially important. Very often, scenes are set before the king, or in the case of Bolingbroke, sometimes the *de facto* king. The king will take a central position, around which the others will place themselves. The deference to the king is sometimes made specific by others' kneeling before him; generally, only the king will be seated. The pattern is so regular that when John of Gaunt is brought on stage in a chair, there may well be an implicit challenge to the king implied in his posture, even before his verbal criticism. Richard represents himself as outraged when Northumberland does not kneel to him at Flint Castle and is bitterly ironic when at the end of the scene Bolingbroke does so, although now Richard is no longer in reality his superior. The indications of what is what in Shakespeare are usually a good deal less subtle.

Yet another special problem with *Richard II* is that it is written entirely in verse, usually of course in what is called blank verse—unrhymed iambic pentameter, basically ten syllables per line with the second, fourth, sixth, eighth, and last more heavily stressed. This is the basic idiom of Shakespearean drama: his characters tend to structure their language this way as a matter of course. The basic effect is to distance the world of his plays from the everyday world of his audiences: Elizabethans did not speak in blank verse. The world on stage is different, heightened, more impressive, usually populated by at least gentry if not nobility and even royalty, sometimes located in an historical or even legendary past. Something of this is immediately established by how much more ornately the people on stage speak than the people in the audience. Often Shakespeare will vary things by having lower-class characters speak prose; but in *Richard II* the only commoners—the gardeners and the groom—speak iambic pentameter. Yet a further complication is that Shakespeare also used rhyme in *Richard II* about 25% of the time, about as heavily as anywhere in his corpus. This is a further distancing device: among the more frequent unrhymed lines, the rhymes call attention to themselves; a pair of rhymed lines often signify the ending of a scene—a kind of signal the audience would be quick to pick up. Rhyme is also often used in Shakespeare to give or to have the speaker give an added sense of significance to what has been said. The deposing of Richard will have enormous effect for the future, and both the author and the characters involved in the on-stage deposition seem to have a sense of what is at stake; the endless rhyming continually underlines its urgency.

A final concern with *Richard II* is the curious relation it has to the question of homosexuality. It should be said immediately that, so far as we know, the historical Richard was not and was not said to be a homosexual. It is also true that, but for a single passage, the play's Richard is not portrayed as a homosexual either. The curious passage occurs in Act 3, scene 1, when Bolingbroke condemns Bushy and Green. He claims

> You have in manner with your sinful hours
> Made a divorce betwixt his queen and him,
> Broke the possession of a royal bed
> And stain'd the beauty of a fair queen's cheeks
> With tears drawn from her eyes by your foul wrongs.   (3.1.11-15)

This sounds as if he is accusing them of having been Richard's homoerotic lovers, although there is no real hint of this elsewhere in the play in Richard's relationships to the favorites and to his queen or in the relationship between the queen and the favorites. It may be that Shakespeare meant simply to have Bolingbroke accuse Bushy and Green of having fostered or directed Richard's licentiousness, for which there is some evidence in the chronicles. Admittedly, one has to emphasize "in manner" rather heavily to support such an explanation. The matter is further complicated by the fact that a couple of years earlier, Christopher Marlowe had written *Edward II*, a history play in which another king (Richard's great-grandfather in fact) dotes on unworthy favorites, alienates his nobility, is deposed, and murdered in prison. Edward II, however, in history and in Marlowe, was the homoerotic lover of his favorites, a matter that outraged his opponents. Marlowe's play was in a number of ways influential upon Shakespeare's, but it is hard to imagine that at this moment, Shakespeare somehow inadvertently substituted Edward's situation for Richard's.

Two of the televised versions considered here, the BBC and the Bard versions, both did a little flirting with the idea of Richard as homosexual by having the actor playing Richard nude or nearly nude in Act 1, scene 4, a private scene between the king and his favorites. Since both versions were prepared for general television broadcast, they hardly could have done more, even if they had wished to. Television, both in the late 70s and early 80s—and to some extent still—was family entertainment sent directly into the homes of the viewers. Until fairly recently a positive or sympathetic presentation of homosexuality as simply a personal and legitimate life-style choice would have been unthinkable. In this regard, the theatrical tradition of *Richard II* was, at least since Gielgud's 1929 performance, far more open to portraying Richard as gay. The Bard production wanted to make a few rather mischievous gestures in that direction. The favorites in this production are dressed in short white tabards, as is Richard, which seems almost a uniform for the group, and something of the contemporary association of homosexuality with effeminacy appears to be hinted at in the flounces, the deeply cut scallops, and the pastel linings of their costumes. They come fairly close to being "campy," and the hats they wear are unmatched outside of Dali.

The avoidance of homosexuality in versions of *Richard II* and this kind of comic, somewhat condescending allusion to it both belong to a long history of changing attitudes that can be understood, if no longer shared. Kittredge's judgment that Shakespeare's Richard II, though frivolous, is not, like Marlowe's Edward II "frankly despicable" is an opinion that belongs to the 1930s.

TIMELINE

1367	Richard born at Bordeaux. He is the son of Edward the Prince of Wales, known as the Black Prince, and the grandson of King Edward III.
1376	Death of the Black Prince.
1377	Death of Edward III; Richard becomes king at the age of ten.
1381	Richard courageously meets with the leaders of the Peasants Revolt and persuades them to withdraw.
1382	Richard marries Anne of Bohemia. It proves to be an affectionate marriage.
c. 1383-85	Richard increasingly at odds with his most powerful nobles because of his reliance on his favorites, especially Michael de la Pole, Earl of Suffolk, and Robert de Vere, Earl of Oxford. His most insistent opponents are the Earl of Arundel, the Earl of Warwick, and especially Thomas of Woodstock, the Duke of Gloucester and Richard's uncle.
1386	The "Wonderful Parliament" imposes a continual council of senior advisors on Richard and dismisses Pole as chancellor.
1387	Richard spends the year attempting to gather military and legal strength to overturn parliament's actions. Richard's opponents defeat an army led by de Vere at Radcot Bridge.
1388	The "Merciless Parliament"—Pole, de Vere, and others "appealed" of treason by Arundel, Warwick, and Gloucester, with two younger men now joining the "lords appellant," Henry Bolingbroke and Thomas Mowbray. Pole and de Vere flee the country, but Richard, under threat of deposition, agrees to the execution of a number of friends and supporters, including Sir Simon Burley, a friend of the Black Prince who had been Richard's tutor as a boy.
1394	Death of Queen Anne.
1394-95	A successful expedition to Ireland; Richard is acknowledged as overlord by the native Irish chieftains.

1396	Richard signs a treaty with Charles VI of France; as part of the treaty Richard marries Charles's six-year-old daughter, Isabel.
1397	Richard proceeds against his old enemies: Arundel is tried and executed, Warwick is exiled, Gloucester is murdered in prison in Calais, seemingly by Richard's order.
1398	The quarrel of Bolingbroke and Mowbray, their aborted duel, and their banishment.
1399	The death of John of Gaunt and Richard's seizure of Bolingbroke's inheritance, Richard's second expedition to Ireland, Bolingbroke's return from exile, Richard's capture on his return from Ireland, Richard's abdication in favor of Bolingbroke, Bolingbroke's coronation as Henry IV.
1400	Richard's murder at Pomfret Castle on February 14.
1564	Birth of William Shakespeare in Stratford.
1582	Shakespeare marries Anne Hathaway.
1592	First, and hostile, notice of Shakespeare in the London theater world as both actor and playwright in Robert Greene's *Groatsworth of Wit*.
1594	Shakespeare a founding member and partner ("sharer") in the Lord Chamberlain's acting company.
1595	Probable date of composition and first performance of *Richard II*.
1596	First quarto of *Richard II*; the play's first appearance in print. (A quarto was a small, cheaply made book, the format in which almost all individual plays were published.)
1597	Second and third quartos of *Richard II* published.
1601	Performance of *Richard II* on the eve of the Earl of Essex's rebellion.
1603	Death of Elizabeth; James I becomes king and the Shakespeare company is taken under his patronage as the King's Men.
1608	Fourth quarto of *Richard II*, the first publication of the full text of the deposition scene (Act 4, scene 1).
c.1613	Shakespeare retires to Stratford.
1616	Death of Shakespeare on April 23.
1623	John Hemings and Henry Condell, Shakespeare's former partners and friends, arrange for the publication of the First Folio, a near complete edition of Shakespeare's plays, eighteen of which now appear in print for the first time

TOPICS FOR DISCUSSION AND FURTHER STUDY

Study Questions

1. In the first scene, is there a significant difference between the quite similar speeches in which Bolingbroke and Mowbray accuse one another?
2. In 1.3, why does Richard stop the duel? Why does he let it proceed to the last moment before stopping it? Why does he exile Mowbray for life, but Bolingbroke for only ten years (later reduced to six)?
3. In 2.1, what relationship does Gaunt's speech on England's heritage of glory have to his criticism of Richard?
4. In 2.3, why does York capitulate to Bolingbroke's return? Does he have other options?
5. In 3.1, is Bolingbroke exceeding his authority in the condemnation of Bushy and Green? Is his condemnation of them just?
6. In 3.2, how many times does Richard fluctuate from total confidence to extreme despair? What do his fluctuations say about him?
7. In 3.3, why does Richard seem to collapse so completely after Northumberland's speech? Are Bolingbroke's protestations of loyalty at the end of the scene sincere or merely a tactic?
8. What new perspective does the discussion of the gardeners in 3.4 give us on the conflict between Richard and Bolingbroke?
9. In 4.1, what would the scene be like if the central section, which was omitted in the first three quartos of the play, were not performed on stage?
10. Is the material about Aumerle's treachery and York's attempt to accuse him comic? Is it out of keeping with the rest of the play?
11. In 5.5, how and how much has Richard changed during his imprisonment?
12. Is Bolingbroke's reaction to the murder of Richard sincere? Is his condemnation of Exton justified?

Performance Questions

1. All or a significant part of the following scenes are cut in at least one of the three television versions: 1.2, 2.2, 2.4, 4.1, 5.2, 5.3. Are these cuts justified? Why are they made?

2. How should the scene at Coventry be played? Is it necessary or desirable to actually put Bolingbroke and Mowbray on their warhorses? How should the seeming delay between Richard exiting with his council and then returning to exile the combatants be played?

3. Focusing especially on 1.4 and 2.2, how should the favorites be played? What shortcomings do they exhibit?

4. Does Bolingbroke in 3.2 actually charge Bushy and Green with having been Richard's homosexual lovers? Is there any evidence in the play to support such a charge? What seems to be their relation to the Queen?

5. In 3.3, does the scene end with Richard as a prisoner? Does this mean that his deposition is already inevitable? Does Richard think so?

6. In the opening of 4.1, Bolingbroke presides over a series of challenges as Richard did in 1.1; does he handle them better or worse than Richard did?

7. At what point in the play, if at all, should Bolingbroke be seated on the throne? At what point should he wear the crown?

BIBLIOGRAPHY

Barrell, Leeds, "A New History for Shakespeare and His Time," *Shakespeare Quarterly*, 39 (1988), 441-64. A discussion of the 1601 Essex performance and of political readings more generally

Berger, Harry, Jr., *Imaginary Audition: Shakespeare on Stage and Page*. Berkeley: University of California Press, 1989. A theatrically aware approach to interpretation that finds Richard unusually astute as a politician.

Brooke, Nicholas. *Shakespeare's Early Tragedies*. London: Methuen, 1968, pp. 107-37. A reading of the play that focuses on four movements rather than the five acts and locates the basis for the tragic outcome in the conflict between royal image and imperfect humanity.

Clamp, Mike, ed., *King Richard II, Cambridge Student Guide*. Cambridge: Cambridge University Press, 2004. A good introduction to the play, its criticism, and the problems of writing about it.

Coyle, Martin, ed., *Shakespeare: Richard II*. Icon Critical Guides. London: Icon Books, 1998. A useful tour through the critical writing on the play including a number of recent and more radical views.

Cubeta, Paul M., ed., *Twentieth Century Interpretation of Richard II*. Englewood Cliffs, N. J., 1971. An excellent collection of the most influential critical essays of the earlier part of the century.

Forker, Charles R., ed. *King Richard II*. Arden 3. London: Arden Shakespeare, 2002. An extremely thorough and reliable scholarly edition; the best currently available.

Hexter, J.H. "Property, Monopoly, and Shakespeare's *Richard II*," in *Culture and Politics from Puritanism to the Enlightenment*, ed. Perez Zagorin. Berkeley: University of California Press, 1980, pp.1-24. An examination of the influences on the play of both the homiletic tradition condemning rebellion and the crucial contemporary interest in inheritance.

Holderness, Brian. "'A Woman's War': A Feminist Reading of Richard II," in *Shakespeare Left and Right*, ed. Ivo Kamps. New York: Routledge, 1991, pp. 167-83. A consideration of the women of the play and the constriction their roles impose upon them.

----------, ed., *Shakespeare's History Plays: Richard II to Henry V.* New Casebook Series. London: Macmillan, 1992. An anthology of criticism with contemporary approaches heavily represented.

Howard, Jean E. and Phyllis Rackin. *Engendering a Nation.* New York: Routledge, 1997. A feminist-materialist reading that explores the meaning of "masculine" and "feminine" in Richard II.

Kantorowicz, Ernst H. *The King's Two Bodies: A Study in Medieval Political Theology.* Princeton: Princeton University Press, 1957. A famous and influential examination of the union and opposition of the human and the divine in the king.

Kott, Jan. *Shakespeare Our Contemporary.* London: Methuen, 1965. An extreme vision of all history, including Shakespeare's, as part of the "Grand Mechanism" of violence and betrayal.

Newlin, Jeanne T., ed., *Richard II: Critical Essays.* New York: Garland Publishing, 1984. A selection of critical essays arranged thematically under "Historical and Political Dynamics," "The Theatre," et al.

Rackin, Phyllis. "The Role of the Audience in Richard II," *Shakespeare Quarterly,* 36 (1985), 262-81. An examination of the play's direction of the audience's sympathies, with special emphasis on the importance of York in this regard.

Righter, Anne. "The Player King," in *Shakespeare and the Idea of the Play.* London: Chatto and Windus, 1962, pp. 102-24. A discussion of the image of the flawed Player King in Shakespeare with particular emphasis on Richard's assuming and rejecting the role.

Saccio, Peter. "Richard II: The Fall of a King," in *Shakespeare's English Kings.* London: Oxford University Press, 1977, pp. 17-35. An exploration of Shakespeare's major variances from the historical record of the reign and his purposes in doing so.

Shewring, Margaret. *King Richard II.* Shakespeare in Performance Series, London: London University Press, 1996. An excellent account of the play on stage from Shakespeare's time to ours.

Tillyard, E.M.W. *Shakespeare's History Plays.* London: Chatto and Windus, 1944. A classic statement of the "Tudor Myth," which saw Richard's deposition as an original sin begetting a century of punishment for England.

Zitner, Sheldon P., "Aumerle's Conspiracy," *Studies in English Literature,* 14 (1974), 239-57. A defense of the often disregarded Aumerle scenes as an ironic commentary on the inflated tonalities of the main action.

A bibliography of *Richard II* on screen

Bulman, J.C., and H.R. Coursen, eds. *Shakespeare on Television: An Anthology of Essays and Reviews.* Hanover, N.H.: University Press of New England, 1988 An extensive collection, especially valuable for contemporary reactions; most useful for the BBC versions.

Forker, Charles R. "Richard II on the Screen'" *Shakespeare Survey,* 61 (2008), 57-73. Reviews the BBC, Bard, and John Farrell versions, as well as the Bogdanov-Pennington ESC.

Grene, Nicholas. "Staging the National Epic." *Shakespeare's Serial History Plays.* Cambridge: Cambridge University Press, 2002, 31-62. Discusses *Age of Kings* and the Hall-Barton and Bogdanov-Pennington stagings of the two tetralogies.

Hattaway, Michael. "Politics and *Mise-en-Scene* in Television Versions of King Richard II." in *Shakespeare on Screen: The Henriad,* ed. Sarah Hatchual and Nathalie Vienne-Guerrin. Rouen: Publications of the Universities of Rouen and Le Havre, pp. 59-74. Commentary on the BBC and Bard versions, as well as the performances of Fiona Shaw and Mark Rylance.

Lennox, Patricia. "An Age of Kings and the 'Normal American,'" *Shakespeare Survey,* 61 (2008), 181-98. Extremely informative on development and reception of the Age of Kings project.

Rothwell, Kenneth S. *A History of Shakespeare on Screen: A Century of Film and Television, 2nd ed.* Cambridge: Cambridge University Press, 1999, 91-118. Valuable comment on a number of televised programs; BBC and Bard versions discussed on pp. 116-18.

Shakespeare, William. *An Age of Kings: The Historical Plays of William Shakespeare as Presented by the British Broadcasting Company's Television Series.* Ed. Nathan Keats and An Keats. New York: Pyramid Books, 1961. The playing text of the televised series; the editors provide brief introductions to each episode.

--------------. *Richard II; The BBC TV Shakespeare.* New York: Mayflower Books, 1978. The text of the BBC version, indicating cuts; valuable introductory essays by Henry Fenwick and Cedric Messina.

FILMOGRAPHY

(*Kings*), *Richard II* (I-"The Hollow Crown"; II-"The Deposing of a King"). Produced for BBC by Peter Dews, directed by Michael Hayes. 1960. Cast: David William (Richard), Tom Fleming (Bolingbroke), Edgar Wreford (Gaunt), Juliet Cooke (Queen), George A. Cooper (Northumberland), Geoffrey Bayldon (York). Running time 60 min. per episode. This *Richard II* was the first two episodes of the fifteen episodes series *William Shakespeare's An Age of Kings*, a pioneering series that dramatized Shakespeare's histories from *Richard II* to *Richard III*, filmed live and in black and white. The series format imposed a fair amount of cutting of the text, and there are, as expected for 1960, some limitations on the camera work. But the direction and acting are both excellent; a very intelligent and enjoyable version.

(*BBC*), *The Complete Dramatic Works of William Shakespeare: Richard II*. Produced by Cedric Messina, directed by William Giles. 1978. Cast: Derek Jacobi (Richard), Jon Finch (Bolingbroke), John Gielgud (Gaunt), Janet Maw (Queen), David Swift (Northumberland), Charles Gray (York). Running time 157 min.This *Richard* was part of the BBC/Time-Life sponsored series, produced in the first year of the series and exemplifying Messina's choice of traditional, non-stylized, realistic staging. The choices work well here, especially because of the remarkable depth of talent of the cast. Despite some complaining at the time, this version had wider resources than the others considered here, as the settings, costumes, and camera work demonstrate. A distinguished version, among the best that Messina and the entire series produced.

(*Bard*), *The Plays of William Shakespeare: King Richard II*. Produced by Jack Nakano, directed by William Woodman. 1981. Cast: David Birney (Richard), Paul Shenar (Bolingbroke), John McLiam (Gaunt), Mary Jane Negro (Queen), John Devlin (Northumberland), Peter MacLean (York). Running time 172 min. This was one of at least nine Shakespeare plays done by Bard Productions Ltd. in California in the early 1980s. Much in response to the BBC plays, the Bard versions were done with American actors, usually television actors, and on a bare stage with rich costumes and no scenery, supposedly to approximate Shakespeare's Globe

Theatre. The acting is competent if occasionally too naturalistic, and the staging is initially interesting, but eventually somewhat constricting. Not a great performance, but clearly worth the watching.

William Shakespeare's Richard the Second. Produced by Joseph Erickson, directed by John Farrell. 2001. Cast: Matte Osian (Richard), Barry Smith (Bolingbroke), Frank O'Donnell (Gaunt), Kadina de Elejalde (Queen), Robert F. McCafferty (Northumberland), David W. Frank (York). Running time 93 minutes. An independent film shot on a disused army installation on an island in Boston Harbor. The deserted structures and overgrown foliage create a sort of post-apocalyptic atmosphere. Accordingly, Farrell dresses his actors (including the women) in contemporary military clothing. Almost everyone is armed, and the cast spends a good deal of time chasing and shooting one another. Presumably, the film's innovations were intended to recompense for its extremely limited material resources. Unfortunately, the direction, acting, photography, and editing are generally amateurish, and this version is of little interest beyond the fact of its eccentricity.